Drug Treatment

Drug Treatment
The Case for Coercion

Sally L. Satel, M.D.

The AEI Press

Publisher for the American Enterprise Institute

WASHINGTON, D.C.

1999

To order call toll free 1-800-462-6420
or 1-717-794-3800. For all other inquiries please contact the AEI
Press, 1150 Seventeenth Street, N.W., Washington, D.C. 20036 or
call 1-800-862-5801.

ISBN 10: 0-8447-7128-7
ISBN 13: 978-0-8447-7128-1

1 3 5 7 9 10 8 6 4 2

THE AEI PRESS
Publisher for the American Enterprise Institute
1150 Seventeenth Street, N.W.
Washington, D.C. 20036

Contents

Acknowledgments

I wish to thank AEI President Christopher DeMuth for welcoming me into the intellectual community of AEI. I am grateful to Douglas Besharov for inviting me to write about this important social issue. A number of people made invaluable editorial suggestions, among them Karlyn Bowman, Suzanne Garment, Christopher DeMuth, and Fred Sommers. My colleagues in the field of substance abuse research and treatment were a generous source of advice and information. They include Dr. Jerome Jaffe, Dr. Robert L. DuPont, Dwayne D. Simpson, Kevin Knight, George W. Joe, Kenneth Silverman, Steve Higgins, Mark Kleiman, Jonathan Caulkins, Faye Taxman, M. Douglas Anglin, Michael Prendergast, David Musto, William L. White, Steven Belenko, Douglas Marlowe, Barry S. Brown, Frank S. Tims, George DeLeon, Norman S. Miller, John Carnevale, Daniel S. Keller, Mitchell Rosenthal, Barbara Lex, James Langenbucher, Douglas Lipton, and Douglas Young. My research on drug courts was supported by the Robert Wood Johnson Foundation.

To judge by the character of the present debate over national drug control policy, an observer would never guess how completely the participants agree about some very important things. The debate is dominated by its extremes, opposing camps that deride each other's arguments. On one side, the "drug warriors," as their critics label them, want to stamp out drug use altogether: They advance strict controls on drug production and harsh punishments for trafficking. At the other end of the continuum, drug legalizers condemn the abolitionist strategy as costly, punitive, and unrealistic, promoting in its place a regime of relaxed controls plus regulation for some or all drugs.

Yet all assent to two crucial points. First, many drug addicts need drug treatment if they are to lead productive and satisfying lives. Second, the more treatment available to each of these addicts, the better. The White House's Office of National Drug Control Policy estimates that the nation's present treatment capacity can accommodate only half the country's 3.5 million addicts,[1] and there is need to narrow the gap.

Why Coercion?

These agreed-on propositions have not been acknowledged for what they are: starting points from which to work toward a policy consensus. The reason for this avoidance is a large, uncomfortable fact. Even if we close the so-called treatment gap, the most promising way—perhaps the only way—to put enough addicts into treatment for long enough to make a difference entails a considerable measure of coercion. This is a proposition massively supported by the empirical data on drug treatment programs, yet it runs counter to some of today's most powerful political and cultural currents.

Data consistently show that treatment, when completed, is quite effective. Indeed, during even brief exposures to treatment, almost all addicts will use fewer drugs and commit less crime than they otherwise would, which means that almost any treatment produces benefits in excess of its cost. But most addicts, given a choice, will not enter a treatment program at all. Those addicts who do enter a program rarely complete it. About half drop out in the first three months, and 80 to 90 percent have left by the end of the first year. Among such dropouts, relapse within a year is the rule.

In short, if treatment is to fulfill its considerable promise as a key component of drug control policy, whether strict or permissive, addicts not only must enter treatment but must stay the course and "graduate." And if they are to do so, most will need some incentives that can properly be considered coercion.

In the context of treatment, the term coercion—used more or less interchangeably with "compulsory treatment," "mandated treatment," "involuntary treatment," "legal pressure into treatment," and "criminal justice referral to treatment"[2]—refers to an array of strategies that shape behavior by responding to specific actions with external pressure and predictable consequences. Coercive drug treatment strategies are already common. Both the criminal justice system and the workplace, for example, have proved to be excellent venues for identifying individuals with drug problems and then exerting leverage, from risk of jail to threat of job loss, to provide powerful incentives to start and stay in treatment.

Moreover, evidence shows that addicts who get treatment through court order or employer mandates benefit as much as, and sometimes more than, their counterparts who enter treatment voluntarily.

This pamphlet presents the case for employing coercion to increase the efficacy of treatment for drug addicts. With the aid of coercion, substance abusers can be rescued earlier in their "careers" of abuse, at a time when intervention can produce greater lifetime benefits. With coercion, more substance abusers will enter treatment than would enroll voluntarily, and those who enroll will enjoy an increased likelihood of success.

The argument will begin by recounting the story of early formal efforts to rehabilitate drug addicts and by drawing the lessons of those efforts. It will proceed to explore modern approaches to coercive treatment and to examine the effectiveness of those approaches. It will then present the sources of current resistance to coercive strategies and, finally, suggest ways to integrate the theory and practice of coercive treatment into current policy.

The aim of the examination is to make the case that unless we acknowledge the necessity for coercive strategies, we will lose the best chance we have for treating addicts in ways that will significantly improve the quality of their lives and that of the society they inhabit.

A Brief History of Coercion in Drug Treatment

America had a perceived drug problem for some fifty years before coercive strategies arose in response.

The Rise of Coercive Treatment. The first wave of cocaine, heroin, and morphine addicts was inadvertently created from the 1880s to the early 1900s, originally by well-meaning physicians, later by hawkers of patent remedies. Most of the resulting "medical addicts," as they were called, were genteel women, personified by the heroin-addicted mother Mary Tyrone in Eugene O'Neill's *Long Day's Journey into Night*. They did not evoke moral censure.

Very different were the addicts who emerged over the first two decades of the twentieth century. These were poor male "pleasure" addicts, harshly condemned as a social menace.[3] In response, the Treasury Department in 1919 cracked down on physicians who prescribed cocaine, heroin, and morphine. States imposed and enforced criminal penalties for use. Officials in big cities, fearing that the hundreds of male addicts thus deprived of their prescriptions would turn in desperation to violent crime, established opiate clinics to dispense morphine and heroin. By 1920, some forty such clinics had been established.

Some of the clinics were worse than ineffective. The most notorious, like the Worth Street Clinic in New York City, were corrupted by their patients' diversion of drugs. The clinics presented the spectacle of bedraggled dope fiends, as the patients were portrayed, loitering around the neighborhood.

The best-run of these facilities, like those in New Haven, Connecticut, Los Angeles, California, and Shreveport, Louisiana, did reduce drug-related crime and illicit trafficking, but they were still unable to point to addicts whom the clinics had cured of their addiction.[4] The Shreveport clinic, however, did keep a close eye on its 198 patients. It maintained meticulous records and required that its addicts hold down jobs and keep up their physical appearance or be cut off from the clinic. This requirement, historian Jill Jonnes notes, "probably weeded out most of the 'sporting' addicts and other unsavory types who so frustrated the New York doctors."[5]

In time, the federal government extended its policy of total drug abstinence to the clinics, which had all closed their doors by 1925. By then all the medical staffs had been threatened with indictment by federal authorities. With the end of this short-lived clinical era, treatment for opiate dependence was largely unavailable between the early 1920s and the end of World War II. Though relatively few new addicts were created during this period, those who had become afflicted in the early 1900s tended to remain opiate-dependent. In particular, a growing population of aging addicts came to inhabit federal prisons, to which addicts convicted of selling or possessing drugs were routinely sent.

Narcotics Farms. As early as 1919, when governments began reining in physicians prescribing the use of opiates, the Narcotics Unit of the Treasury Department urged Congress to set up a series of federal narcotics farms where users could be confined and treated.[6] It wasn't until 1935, however, in response to the problem of aging addicts, that the U.S. Public Health Service opened a facility in Lexington, Kentucky. Three years later another federal farm was established in Fort Worth, Texas. These facilities received both criminal violators and addicts who enrolled in treatment voluntarily.

The Lexington facility was a hospital-prison-sanitarium in which medical and moral approaches to treatment converged. It was located, as Jonnes has described it,

> on 1,100 acres of rolling bluegrass. . . . an Art Deco campus-like affair with barred windows. In its early years, Lexington was literally a working farm operated by patient-inmates with chicken hatcheries, slaughter houses, four large dairy barns, a green house and a utility barn. When not farming, inmates could work in sewing, printing or wood working shops.[7]

The facilities did not, however, succeed in providing a wholesome and salutary rural respite. According to Jonnes, the "effect of going to KY [as patient-inmates called the Lexington farm] for most addicts was to expand their network of addict pals." The doctors were dedicated but frustrated, often noting that their patients would likely relapse upon returning to the inner cities from which they came.

The data confirmed the doctors' impressions. According to a report by the U.S. comptroller general, approximately 70 percent of the hospital's voluntary patients signed out against medical advice before completing the six-to-twelve–month treatment program; and within a few years, 90 percent had relapsed.[8] Most who remained in treatment did so under legal pressure from a court.

Still, though the farms are generally considered to have been failures, they generated useful clinical information. Most important, several follow-up studies of the participants indicated that addicts who after treatment were supervised under legal coercion had better outcomes than those not so supervised. A follow-up of more than 4,000 addicts six months after discharge from treatment found that those on probation or parole were more than twice as likely to remain abstinent as were voluntary patients, probably because the former had compulsory post-hospital supervision.[9] A longer-term follow-up of the same population confirmed the critical role of post-hospital surveillance: it found that of those serving more than twelve months of parole, 67 percent remained drug-free a year after discharge, while the figure for voluntary patients was only 4 percent.[10]

The data showed, in sum, that some kind of post-discharge supervision was needed. The information also yielded the lessons that (a) a six-to-twelve–month treatment stay was too brief; (b) the need was for intensive vocational services rather than for psychological services aimed at personality change; and (c) the threat of reinstitutionalization had to have teeth.

Therapeutic Communities. After World War II, organized crime was able to reactivate the old heroin trafficking routes disrupted by the war, and inner-city physicians began to encounter the next generation of heroin addicts. Therefore the 1950s saw a resurgence of interest in the treatment of addiction—and in particular, the emergence of the notion of the self-regulating therapeutic community (TC). This concept was enthusiastically welcomed by clinicians and policymakers alike, who were heartened by early TC success stories and demoralized by the gloomy results of previous treatment efforts.

The idea of a therapeutic community was exemplified by Synanon, a residential facility established by former alcoholic Charles Dederich in Santa Monica, California, to treat both alcohol and heroin addicts. Synanon was followed by the establishment in New York City of Daytop Village and, in 1967, of Phoenix House. The latter, a residential center on the Upper West Side, was founded by psychiatrist Mitchell Rosenthal. It was inspired by the efforts of six former addicts who enlisted Dr. Rosenthal's help in their commitment to keep themselves clean.

Modern therapeutic communities immerse patients in a comprehensive eighteen-to-twenty-four–month treatment regimen built around the philosophy that the addict's primary problem is not the drug he abuses but the addict himself. Though psychiatric orthodoxy holds that addiction is a discrete, self-contained "disease," the therapeutic community's approach recognizes drug abuse as a symptom of a deeper personal disturbance. The strategy for rehabilitation is to transform the destructive patterns of feeling, thinking, and acting that predispose a person to use drugs.

In this effort, the primary "therapist" is the community itself—not only peers but also staff members, some of whom are graduates of a program themselves and can serve as role models. The dynamic is mutual self-help; residents continually reinforce, for each other, the expectations and rules of the community. For meeting community expectations, residents win rewards—privileges like weekend passes or increasing responsibility, culminating in leadership roles. If a resident defies the rules, he or she loses privileges and must perform the least desirable chores. All residents must work—above all so that they learn to accept authority and supervision, vital to their future success in the work force.

Researcher George DeLeon has identified three stages in a resident's attitude toward such communities:[11]

1. compliance: adherence to rules simply to avoid negative consequences such as disciplinary action, discharge from the program, or reincarceration
2. conformity: adherence to the recovery community's norms to avoid loss of approval or disaffiliation
3. commitment: development of a personal determination to change destructive attitudes and behaviors

Those who negotiate the commitment stage have excellent outcomes. De Leon, in a long-term follow-up study of addicts admitted to Phoenix House, found that after five to seven years, 90 percent of those who had graduated were employed and crime-free, and 70 percent were drug-free.[12]

But the graduates constituted only 20 percent of De Leon's sample. Generally, half of voluntarily committed patients leave therapeutic communities prematurely within the first ninety days, the threshold at which most individuals form an independent commitment to a treatment program. Perhaps one in five to ten fully completes a program.[13]

These dropout rates are not hard to understand. In the early months of a program, residents of a therapeutic community often rebel against the rigid structure, loss of status they enjoyed on the street, and deprivation of getting high. Ambivalence about relinquishing drugs is a powerful psychological force pulling patients back to the street. Even patients with strong motivation experience flagging resolve, momentary disillusionment, or intense cravings. If a patient succumbs to these pressures and leaves treatment prematurely, he or she may have gained some benefit from even the brief exposure to treatment but is at high risk for relapse into drug use and crime.

De Leon therefore sees legal pressure as the initial force that can literally get patients through the door into treatment and keep them there until they internalize the values and goals of recovery. Coercion alone cannot do the job: one researcher observed that "if contact with therapy does not bring its own rewards, the potency of coercion will decline precipitously, and could ultimately work against treatment goals."[14] But the threat of consequences like incarceration, the loss of a job, or some other aversive event can sustain an ambivalent or flatly resistant patient during the early months of treatment until those rewards—newly learned skills, a transformed self-concept, social maturation, and optimism about the future—ultimately inspire him or her to change.

Thus it is of interest that in De Leon's Phoenix House sample, it did not matter statistically to a patient's chances of "graduating" whether he or she had enrolled voluntarily or been mandated to treatment.[15] This similarity did not mean, in De Leon's view, that compelled treatment made no difference; it was just the opposite. The compelled patients began with worse prognoses, because of their legal involvement and their higher incidence of antisocial personality disorder and low motivation.[16] Counteracting these disadvantages, however, was the fact that individuals who had court cases pending or had been legally referred to the community spent, on average, more days in treatment than did voluntary patients.[17] The relatively bad prognosis was made up for by more treatment days. "Retention in treatment," De Leon therefore concluded, "is the best predictor of outcome, and legal referral is a consistent predictor of retention."

Methadone. The postwar period also saw, in the early 1960s, a renewed receptiveness to the idea of drug maintenance. The number of heroin users was increasing, and the treatment available to New York City's 100,000 heroin addicts—half of those in the nation—remained limited to hospital-based detoxification and the Daytop Lodge therapeutic community. A few years earlier, a joint committee of the American Bar Association and the American Medical Association had called for restoring physicians' freedom to prescribe heroin and for the establishment of an experimental clinic for this purpose. In 1963, both the New

York Academy of Medicine and President John F. Kennedy's Presidential Commission on Narcotic and Drug Abuse (the Prettyman Commission) made similar recommendations.[18]

Marie Nyswander and Vincent Dole, physicians at New York's Rockefeller Institute, set out to develop new pharmacological approaches to treating heroin addiction. They hypothesized that suppressing the physiological craving for the drug was the key to treating the addiction, and they sought a replacement or "substitution" drug that would, unlike heroin and morphine, not wear off within a few hours. Ideally, a long-acting medication would stabilize individuals so that they could hold down a job and function normally.

Nyswander and Dole chose methadone, a long-acting synthetic opiate developed by German chemists searching for an inexpensive morphine-like medicine during World War II. Addicts could take methadone orally and needed to do so only once a day to prevent withdrawal and craving. Moreover, because methadone worked by blocking opiate receptors, patients would not experience euphoria even if they took heroin in addition.

Dole started six patients on methadone in 1965. Around the same time, the United States experienced an influx of heroin from the Golden Triangle of Burma, Laos, and Thailand, fueling an epidemic that peaked in most American cities between 1969 and 1972. By 1969 almost 2,000 New York City addicts were enrolled in Dole's maintenance clinic, and by 1970 the city had expanded the clinic system to serve 20,000 voluntary patients.[19]

There are not many studies of the relationship between compelled treatment and methadone therapy because, though methadone is one of the best-studied anti-addiction therapies to date, few patients are legally mandated to maintenance treatment. The major source of compelled treatment, the criminal justice system, prefers rehabilitation that aims for total abstinence rather than substitution of one dependence-producing agent for another.

More than twenty years ago, however, M. Douglas Anglin of the University of California, Los Angeles, conducted an important study to determine whether addicts coerced into drug treatment differed from voluntary patients in their responses to treatment.[20] Anglin categorized some 600 methadone-maintenance patients according to whether they were subject to high, moderate, or low levels of coercion. The 19 percent in the high-level category were under official legal supervision, including required urine testing, and perceived their entry into treatment as motivated primarily by the legal system. Another 19 percent, moderately coerced, were under active legal supervision and either were submitting to urine tests or perceived coercion as the reason for their entry into treatment. Finally, 62 percent of the sample, under a low level of coercion, were not under legal supervision and not subject to monitoring via probation or parole. The majority of these reported feeling no legal pressure, even as minor as a fear of arrest, impelling them toward treatment.

When Anglin compared the three groups, he found that all of them showed substantial improvement when measured on narcotics use, crime, and social functioning. Once again, compelling patients to accept treatment did not bar clinical progress; given the relatively poor prognoses of those involved, it probably aided such progress.

The same lesson emerged from a more recent experience with methadone treatment at the Southeast Baltimore Drug Treatment program. A research team led by psychologist Michael Kidorf of Johns Hopkins University noted that unemployment was a common problem among inner-city drug users and lamented that "standard drug abuse treatment services appear to have only small effects on employment."[21] In response the Baltimore clinic, like its predecessor clinic in Shreveport some seventy years earlier, instituted the once-again-innovative requirement that its methadone patients be employed for at least twenty hours a week in order to receive methadone and related services. Patients were given two months to find employment or to enroll in job training or community service programs. If they did not, they received five weeks of intensive counseling. Those who did not obtain employment after counseling were tapered off methadone.

Because these patients had been enrolled in the same clinic before the requirement went into effect, their performance prior to the new rule could be compared with the same population's performance afterward. Before the requirement, despite enhanced counseling with vocational training, none had managed to secure either paying or volunteer employment. Two months after the imposition of the requirement, however, 75 percent of the sample had secured and maintained verified paid employment, volunteer work, or education.

Civil Commitment. Compelled treatment showed its potential in the California Civil Addict program, created in 1961 as the first-implemented statewide civil commitment program in the country. Serving mostly heroin addicts, the program flourished during the 1960s.[22] The California Department of Corrections ran the program, providing high-quality treatment by specifically recruited and specially trained corrections personnel.

During the program's most active years, its protocol included an average of eighteen months of inpatient treatment out of a total commitment period of seven years. After eighteen to twenty-four months in residential treatment, patients spent up to five years being closely supervised by specially trained parole officers with small caseloads, who monitored patients closely and administered weekly urine toxicology tests. For any narcotics use violation discovered by these tests, the officers had authority to take action—including returning patients for treatment to the institutions from which they had been discharged.

This program became the venue for an unfortunate natural experiment. During the program's first two years, judges and other officials unfamiliar with its procedures

mistakenly released about half of the committed population after only minimal exposure to the inpatient part of
the program. Anglin's research team took advantage of
this circumstance, selecting a sample of individuals who
had participated in the program's inpatient treatment for
a sustained length of time and comparing it with a
matched sample of individuals who had been erroneously
released. The team compared the two groups on their self-
reported percentages of time spent on drug use and criminal activity, then verified the data through arrest records
and urine specimens taken at follow-up interviews.

By one year after the premature release of half the
study population, the two groups had sharply diverged.
Individuals who had been prematurely released were more
than twice as likely as those who had completed eighteen
months as inpatients to use narcotics. During the subsequent years of outpatient supervision, narcotics use declined for both groups; but the decline for those who had
been kept as inpatients averaged 22 percent, while the
figure for the discharged group was only 7 percent.

Criminal activity followed a similar pattern. Before
commitment, both groups had devoted about 60 percent
of their time to such activity. A year after one group had
been prematurely discharged, the figure for the treated
group was 20 percent, while the figure for the discharged
group was 48 percent. At the end of seven years, criminal
activity among the treated group had undergone a further reduction of 19 percent, but the reduction figure for
the discharged group was only 7 percent.

New York followed California's model, with a crucial
and deleterious difference. Prompted by California's success, New York began its own civil commitment program
in 1966. New York had the advantage of that year's federal Narcotic Addict Rehabilitation Act, which aimed to
link criminal justice agencies to community-based treatment programs. The act provided for compulsory treatment for addicts charged with certain nonviolent federal
crimes; for treatment instead of sentencing for those con-

victed of such crimes; and for voluntary commitment of drug users not involved in criminal proceedings. The act also began what was to become, in the 1970s, massive federal funding of treatment programs.

But New York—unlike California, which mandated addicts to rehabilitation—allowed addicts to choose between treatment and incarceration. Those who chose the former were treated in residential settings developed during those years by the state Narcotics Addiction Control Commission, but this phase of treatment lasted only about nine months. Inpatient treatment was followed by parole-like supervision for another two to four years. Unfortunately, supervision was loose, and a high percentage of patients went AWOL. Governor Nelson Rockefeller was, not surprisingly, discouraged. "Let's be frank," he said in his 1973 Address to the Legislature; "we have achieved very little permanent rehabilitation, we have found no cure."[23]

Modern Evaluations of the Effectiveness of Compelled Treatment

Throughout the 1960s the heroin epidemic continued, along with increasing rates of crime and deaths from overdose. Heroin addiction among servicemen in Vietnam compounded national anxiety about the drug problem, raising the specter of a country inundated with returning soldiers hooked on narcotics. There were long waiting lists for treatment, and politicians were forced to confront the inadequacy of the system.

In June 1971, President Nixon declared the first "war on drugs." He created the Special Action Office for Drug Abuse Prevention (SAODAP), precursor of the office of today's "drug czar." The new director of SAODAP, Jerome Jaffe, emphasized that "its implication as a landmark in the area of treatment should not be minimized. For the first time in the history of the Nation there was an explicit commitment to make treatment readily available."[24]

Federal treatment resources expanded rapidly. In 1969, 6 community mental health-drug treatment centers were in operation. Four years later, there were 300 such programs, and by 1977 there were more than 3,000.[25] The programs were of four types:

1. *Inpatient.* This term describes programs in which a patient enters a hospital or free-standing facility for a few days to a few weeks, often beginning with several days to a week, depending on the abused drug, for detoxification. The aim is to break the cycle of use physiologically, to stabilize the patient psychiatrically, and to arrange for longer-term outpatient or residential treatment.[26]

2. *Outpatient (drug-free).* This treatment ranges from one or two counseling visits per week, or several weekly visits including group therapy, to intensive versions offering daily sessions. Patients learn how to identify and avoid triggers for drug craving and use and to handle drug cravings. They are typically referred to community agencies for health, mental health, educational, vocational, legal, and other needed services.[27]

3. *Methadone maintenance.* This treatment foresees extended dependence on heroin and other opiates. A daily oral dose of methadone, a long-acting narcotic, acts as a heroin substitute, blocking the physical withdrawal and craving associated with abrupt discontinuation of heroin. Patients may be maintained on methadone for many years, depending on individual needs. High-quality programs offer rehabilitative services. Some use newer maintenance medications, such as LAAM (levo-alpha acetylmethadol), which has the advantage of being longer-acting than methadone, or buprenorphine, which has the advantage of being less addictive.[28]

4. *Therapeutic communities.* These residential programs involve stays of six to twenty-four months, phasing into more independent residential living. The programs are highly structured: patients progress through a hierarchy of occupational training and community responsi-

bilities. The goals are to resocialize patients and enable them to develop stable relationships.[29]

National Outcome Studies. The first evaluation of this network of community-based programs began in 1968, when the National Institute of Mental Health funded a proposal by Saul B. Selis, director of the Institute of Behavioral Research at Texas Christian University, for the Drug Abuse Reporting Project (DARP). Data collection began in 1969 and lasted four years, following about 44,000 patients enrolled in fifty-two federally funded programs. The project followed subgroups for five and twelve years following discharge from treatment.

In 1974, the institute transferred control of the project to the newly created National Institute on Drug Abuse (NIDA). NIDA subsequently funded two more large studies: the Treatment Outcome Prospective Study (TOPS), which followed 12,000 patients who entered treatment between 1979 and 1981, and the Drug Abuse Treatment Outcome Study (DATOS), which followed 11,000 patients who entered between 1991 and 1993. More recently another federal agency, the Center for Substance Abuse Treatment, undertook the National Treatment Improvement and Evaluation Study of 4,400 patients who entered the project between 1993 and 1995.

Taken together, these studies assessed roughly 70,000 patients, of whom 40 to 50 percent were court-referred or otherwise mandated to residential and outpatient treatment programs.[30]

Two major findings emerged from these huge evaluations. The first was that the length of time a patient spent in treatment was a reliable predictor of his or her posttreatment performance. Beyond a ninety-day threshold, treatment outcomes improved in direct relationship to the length of time spent in treatment, with one year generally found to be the minimum effective duration of treatment.[31]

The second major finding was that coerced patients tended to stay longer. (On this second point, DARP was an exception, finding no correlation between criminal justice status and either time spent in treatment or improvement. One can say only that DARP's compelled patients stayed as long as, and did no worse than, voluntary patients.)

To evaluate these findings, it is important to know whether addicts who entered treatment under legal coercion were meaningfully different from other patients. The findings from these studies are mixed. Some show that legally coerced addicts had a relatively unfavorable preadmission profile—more crime and gang involvement, more drug use, worse employment records than had their noncoerced counterparts. Other studies detected little difference other than the particular offense that triggered the mandate to treatment.[32]

In the DARP study, the baseline characteristics of voluntary and legally referred patients were similar. Because the subjects were relatively homogeneous on these dimensions—being primarily young, male, inner-city "street addicts," more than 80 percent with at least one previous arrest, and more than half previously incarcerated—the authors speculate that legal status was unlikely to have been a very discriminating variable.

The TOPS study, by contrast, discovered some differences. True, legally mandated and voluntary patients alike had similar drug use patterns, comparable previous criminal justice involvement, and equivalent numbers of prior treatment episodes. But the legally mandated patients were younger than their voluntary counterparts and more likely to be male. When researchers looked specifically at patients who reported that the criminal justice system was the primary source of their referral to treatment, they found that these legal referrals not only were younger but also used mainly alcohol and marijuana rather than "harder" drugs. The authors speculate that the legally mandated patients were "caught" earlier in their careers, or that they were incarcerated too recently to have reestablished their habits, or both.

Although the studies do not present a consistent picture of pretreatment characteristics of legally mandated patients, they do make it reasonable to conclude that even legally coerced addicts having relatively unfavorable prognoses can benefit from treatment as much as voluntary patients can, since the latter often remain in treatment for a shorter period.[33]

A 1990 report from the Institute of Medicine summarized that "contrary to earlier fears among clinicians, criminal justice pressure does not seem to vitiate treatment effectiveness, and it probably improves retention."[34] Thus, while there is conflicting evidence on whether a legal mandate brings individuals into treatment earlier, coercion can almost surely be credited with derailing many an addiction career once individuals have been brought into treatment.[35]

Of special significance, in light of the importance of length of treatment, is the fact that all four national outcome studies showed high rates of attrition among patients, with half dropping out inside of ninety days. For these early dropouts, the benefits of treatment disappeared within the year. With substantial, durable change rarely occurring in less than a year or two of treatment, the high dropout rate makes retaining patients in treatment a pressing challenge.

Some researchers have hypothesized that the key to retention is to match each individual patient with the proper type of treatment. Although in principle such matching makes clinical and economic sense, there is surprisingly little tested information about such attempts. Two prospective studies by A. Thomas McLellan of the University of Pennsylvania suggest that tailoring patient care can indeed make a difference.[36] McLellan assigned patients to programs according to particular psychiatric, medical, or family needs and found better outcomes for these patients than for those without such treatment. One of the national outcomes studies, DATOS, similarly found that even severely drug-dependent patients were more likely to be abstinent at their one-year follow-up if they had received support services targeted to specific needs.

But these findings are not uniform. The American Society for Addiction Medicine has developed widely used criteria for placing patients in specific treatment modalities; the few studies assessing the validity of these criteria, however, have not found an effect on outcomes.[37]

Thus far it appears that "patient matching," while it may be one means of assigning patients to treatment, is no substitute for length of treatment. It is length of exposure to treatment that powerfully predicts patient success, no matter what the treatment setting. The federal Center for Substance Abuse Treatment, in a recent study examining the relationship between these two variables, compared one sample of addicts who had ten months of residential care followed by two months of outpatient care with another sample who had six months of residential care followed by another six months of outpatient care. Regardless of the treatment scheme to which patients were assigned, those who completed the entire twelve-month treatment period had the best outcomes. And those most likely to complete the course of treatment were patients under probation, parole, or pretrial supervision.[38]

Treatment Alternatives to Street Crime. TASC, established as a federal program in 1972 as one of the first initiatives of the Nixon administration's war on drugs, was moderately successful in cutting the number of street crimes committed by addicts. TASC was meant to serve as a bridge between the criminal justice and treatment systems. It functioned as a diversion program for drug abusers, diverting them from jail or prison by identifying nonviolent addicted criminals and referring them to treatment in the community. TASC assigned arrestees to case managers who were to get them into treatment and send progress reports back to the courts. The program, now supported primarily by state and local governments, subsequently expanded to supervising probationers and to post-sentencing disposition.

TASC has been the subject of a number of evaluations. Most are positive; others are partly so. In one such study, the TOPS project compared a subgroup of TASC-referred patients with a group of voluntary, unmonitored patients involved in the criminal justice system.[39] Comparing patients' drug use one year before treatment with their drug use after the first three to six months of treatment, the TOPS researchers found that the TASC patients' use had declined by 81 percent; the comparable figure for the control group was 74 percent. Predatory illegal acts had declined by 96 percent for the TASC group, but only by 71 percent for the control group.

The Education and Assistance Corporation analyzed results from the Brooklyn, New York, TASC program.[40] Of 173 felons placed in treatment in 1992, 71 percent remained in the program for at least two years. At twenty-nine months after completion of the program, the group's rearrest rate was 9 percent. This was much lower than either the 25 percent rearrest rate among offenders from a control program or the 28 percent rearrest rate among the general inmate population in New York State correctional facilities.

In Texas, a study found that 7 percent of TASC-referred offenders were incarcerated during an eighteen-month observation period, compared with 28 percent of offenders who did not enter treatment or who stayed fewer than three months.[41]

Finally, researchers at UCLA and RAND studying five regional sites compared TASC offenders mandated to treatment or to surveillance, including urine testing and case management, with a control group of offenders who received standard probation with little supervision.[42] The TASC and control groups were similar on most demographic, drug, and criminal-record variables. At six months after patients' entry into the study, the researchers measured police-confirmed new arrests and technical violations, along with unverified self-reports of drug use.

The findings varied across the sites. In three places, TASC patients showed greater reductions in all three outcomes. In some places there was no difference in one or another outcome. At two sites, Birmingham, Alabama, and Portland, Oregon, the researchers actually found more criminal involvement and technical violations among TASC patients—but the authors attributed this phenomenon to the fact that the TASC offenders were being watched more closely and were thus more likely to get caught. (The authors also thought that the figures on self-reported drug use among TASC patients might be artificially low because heavily monitored groups might be more likely to minimize their reporting of punishable behavior.)

Coercion of Criminals. An estimated 60 percent of the cocaine and heroin used in the United States is consumed by the 5 million Americans who are supervised by or incarcerated within the criminal justice system. Moreover, offenders who abuse drugs are more likely than nonabusing offenders to return to crime following release from incarceration.[43] Therefore there is considerable potential within the criminal justice system for reducing drug abuse and related crime by mandated treatment. Evidence indicates that diversionary and in-prison treatment programs, although currently available only to some 15 percent of offenders, have a benefit beyond the crime-reducing effects of incarceration or probation as usual.[44] Results from several categories of criminal commitment show that treated offenders have lower rates of recidivism. Although these studies do not always directly measure post-treatment drug use, crime itself can reasonably be used as indirect evidence of drug involvement, since the two activities are so highly correlated. Conversely, declines in drug use are accompanied by declines in crime, particularly income-generating crime.[45]

Drug courts. One major category of coerced treatment of criminals occurs in drug courts, which offer nonviolent offenders, usually recidivists, the prospect of dismissed charges if they plead guilty and agree to be diverted to a heavily monitored drug treatment and testing program overseen by a judge. Although in the TASC model judges do not have direct contact with treatment personnel, a drug court is a hub from which services such as treatment, case management, and vocational training radiate.[46]

Drug courts originated in southern Florida in the late 1980s, when the area was hit hard by cocaine-related arrests that flooded courtrooms and overwhelmed jails. Addicts out on probation were quickly rearrested for new drug-related crimes, and the revolving door to the justice system seemed to be spinning out of control. Drug courts promised a way to break the cycle by "reserving" jail and prison beds for dangerous offenders while sending criminally involved addicts to treatment. The first one opened in Miami in 1989.

Enthusiasm about drug courts has spawned a drug court movement. Today, according to the National Association of Drug Court Professionals, there are almost 300 drug courts in operation, up from about 20 in 1994. An estimated 90,000 individuals have been enrolled. As of spring 1998, every state but Rhode Island had at least one drug court in operation. California, where nearly a quarter of all state prisoners are incarcerated because of a drug offense, has more than 70.

Although the accumulated evidence of drug courts' effectiveness has yet to reach a critical threshold because only a handful of independently evaluated studies have been performed, the early data look promising. More than 70 percent of drug court participants have been incarcerated at least once previously, almost three times more than have been in drug treatment;[47] thus for many offenders, drug court is the route of entry into rehabilitation. In almost all drug courts, retention in court-ordered drug treatment is consistently several times greater than it is in voluntary treatment.[48]

A General Accounting Office (GAO) report found that the average retention rate of drug court programs was a highly respectable 71 percent. Even the lowest retention rate that the GAO found in a drug court, 31 percent, exceeds the average one-year retention rate of some 15 percent for noncriminal addicts in public-sector treatment programs.[49] This comparison is all the more impressive in light of the fact that the criminally involved addict is generally considered the hardest to treat in conventional settings. The GAO report also found, like other studies, that the longer a participant stayed in drug court treatment, the better he or she fared.

A survey by the Drug Court Clearinghouse at American University found similar patterns. Survey results first emphasized the element of coercion in drug court participation. Although 80 percent of offenders who were offered the drug court option chose to take it, many saw it simply as an expeditious way to get their charges dropped. Indeed, some actually said they planned to return to drugs after they "went through the motions" in the program.[50]

Yet the survey also found that drug courts operational for eighteen months or more reported completion rates of 48 percent. Rearrest rates, primarily for drug crimes, varied according to graduates' characteristics and degree of social dysfunction, but they averaged just 4 percent at one year after graduation. Even among those who failed to finish the program, rearrest rates one year after enrollment ranged from 28 percent down to 5 percent. By contrast, the Bureau of Justice Statistics reports a 26 to 40 percent rearrest rate for individuals convicted of drug possession who are traditionally adjudicated.[51]

Evaluations of particular drug courts also show good results. The Portland, Oregon, drug court was evaluated in 1998 by the State Justice Institute, which made careful efforts to match drug court participants with other arrestees having similar demographic characteristics and criminal histories who had either refused drug court or were ineligible for administrative reasons. Two years after adjudication, drug court program participants had 61 percent fewer arrests than had offenders who were eligible but did not participate. Drug court graduates performed best, with 76 percent fewer arrests two years later. The longer the retention, the better the outcomes: those who stayed for less than one-third of the program duration had three times as many arrests as had those who graduated, and twice as many as those who completed at least one-third.[52]

The Maricopa, Arizona, drug court was the subject of a 1996 evaluation by RAND, which found that among a sample randomly assigned to the drug court, rates of rearrest for any crime were significantly lower than for those randomly assigned to probation alone.[53]

A recent review of the Broward County, Florida, drug court found that drug court graduates were half as likely to be rearrested for a felony, and one-third as likely to be rearrested for a drug felony, as demographically similar offenders who were eligible for drug court but had instead chosen and completed probation.[54]

An independent evaluation found the Dade County, Florida, drug court superior to "disposition as usual."[55] Between June 1989 and March 1993, the Dade County program enrolled 4,500 defendants, 20 percent of all arrestees in the county who were charged with drug-related offenses. During that same period, 60 percent of the enrollees graduated or remained in the program. A year after graduation, only 11 percent were rearrested in Dade County on any criminal charge. By contrast, the rearrest rate was some 60 percent for a matched sample of drug offenders in 1987, two years before institution of the drug court. Furthermore, the time that elapsed between graduation and first reoffense was two to three times longer in the drug court group than in the nondrug court group.

In the most mixed evaluation of results in a drug court, the Urban Institute found that participants randomly assigned to the District of Columbia drug court from 1993 to 1995 were twice as likely to be drug free in the month before sentencing as those assigned to probation as usual; the figures were 27 percent versus 12 percent.[56]

Six months after sentencing, however, rearrest rates for any crime averaged 4 percent for the treatment track versus 6 percent for the control track, not a statistically significant difference.

Prison-based programs. Approximately 70 percent of all state prison inmates are in need of substance abuse treatment.[57] Reporting states indicated, however, that only 15 percent completed a prescribed substance-abuse–treatment program before their release from confinement.[58]

About 12 percent of prisons have intensive treatment programs based on therapeutic community principles,[59] lasting from six to fifteen months and open to nonviolent offenders who are within eighteen months of eligibility for work release or parole. Within the prison, these offenders are segregated from the rest of the inmate population, in order to maintain the integrity of the program and to protect participants from other prisoners.

In a comprehensive review of the prison-based programs of the 1970s and 1980s, Falkin and coauthors concluded that in-prison therapeutic communities are effective.[60] Examining programs such as New York's Stay'n Out (which they praised as a national model), Oregon's Cornerstone Program, and others, the authors found that the treatment experience, optimally sustained for nine to twelve months, was strongly correlated with successful subsequent parole. For example, violations of parole occurred among 50 percent of the offenders who stayed for less than three months in Stay'n Out; among 39 percent of those who stayed longer than three months; and among only 15 percent of those who completed the program. Reincarceration rates within three years of release from prison were significantly lower for Stay'n Out participants, no matter how long they participated, than for matched offenders who had expressed interest in being treated but did not meet technical eligibility requirements.

Similarly, Cornerstone graduates had a 36 percent reincarceration rate over a three-year follow-up period, while the figure was 63 percent for parolees-as-usual. The graduates' relative success occurred despite the fact that they had begun with more severe criminal and substance abuse histories than had the control group.

Work release. In 1987, the Delaware Department of Corrections established the Crest program, the first therapeutic community work-release center in the United States.[61] Offenders who had been released from prison after participating in the Key program, a prison-based therapeutic community for drug-involved offenders at a maximum security prison, entered the Crest Center for three months of on-site treatment, three months of additional treatment, and job training, also within a therapeutic community.

Led by the center's director, James Inciardi, researchers from the University of Delaware's Center for Drug and Alcohol Studies compared four groups of mostly male participants: Key participants who did not go on to Crest; Crest participants who had not gone through the Key program; Key and Crest combined; and a control group that had first been incarcerated without treatment, then had gone on to conventional work release. The Key and Key-Crest groups had begun with higher levels of drug abuse and longer criminal histories. The Key-only group was older and less likely to be white.

The study found that the longer a participant's tenure in treatment was and the closer to time of release the treatment was received, the better the post-release outcome. In sum, the therapeutic element of the prison-parole combination appears to reside more heavily in the parole phase than in the incarceration.

At an early follow-up, in-prison treatment was found to be somewhat more beneficial than no treatment. By eighteen months, however, there was no significant difference between the Key and control groups in rearrest rates and urinalysis-confirmed drug use. By contrast, at eighteen months Crest-only participants maintained an advantage over the control group. In addition, at the six-month follow-up, the Crest group was as successful as the Key-Crest group; but by eighteen months, the Key-Crest group was superior, with 77 percent arrest-free and 47 percent drug-free among Key-Crest participants, while the figures were only 57 percent arrest-free and 31 percent drug-free among the Crest group.

The Key-Crest combination outranked all the others, with nearly half the individuals being drug-free at eighteen months, a figure three times higher than that of the control group, while Crest-only participants had an intermediate likelihood of being drug-free.

Diversion from prison. In 1990, the office of the Kings County (Brooklyn) District Attorney developed the Drug Treatment Alternative to Prison (DTAP) program in response to the increasing pressure of drug-related commitments on the state prison system. (By the mid-1990s, drug offenders would constitute nearly one-half of admissions to state prisons.) The program diverts nonviolent drug felons to long-term, community-based residential drug treatment at about two-thirds the cost of incarceration. Like drug court, the program offers dismissal of charges in return for an offender's completing treatment under close judicial supervision. Also like drug court, DTAP may be chosen by offenders for reasons having little to do with a desire to become drug-free. For some, the program is a way to avoid incarceration; for others, it promises an expunged criminal record.

The Vera Institute of Justice in New York City has conducted an independent evaluation of DTAP.[62] Vera found that participants began with more severe pretreatment deficits—in education, employment, and legal involvement—than those of offenders placed in other diversion programs. Yet DTAP's total retention rate at one year was 64 percent, two to four times higher than that of residential programs in general. At one year, 11 percent of DTAP participants had been rearrested, half for drug offenses; by comparison, drug offenders sent to prison are more than twice as likely to be rearrested within a year of release, with more than half those arrests being drug-related. Fewer than 5 percent of ex-prisoners are rearrested while in treatment, but dropouts have high rates of reoffense, ranging from 80 to 92 percent, with an average time before return to custody of only one week.

Coercion without Treatment

Practical experience suggests that simply diverting addicts to monitoring systems may be sufficient incentive to improved behavior for those with relatively low levels of drug involvement. This proposition has not, however, been rigorously tested. Whether drug testing and sanctions alone can lead to abstinence or near-abstinence in certain offenders is an important question for several reasons. First, some offenders will inevitably, if choice is available, opt for routine processing with a short, fixed period of incarceration over a diversionary program that requires long periods of supervision and threatens reincarceration if they backslide. Second, the supervision associated with standard probation, or even sometimes with parole, lasts for just months, as compared with the years-long average duration of a career of addiction, and is of only low intensity. Finally, even among offenders who do choose treatment or are mandated into it, some might be successfully managed with less expensive forms of monitoring.

A few jurisdictions, instead of specifically mandating treatment, are extending the heightened supervision typical of diversionary programs to larger numbers of offenders for longer periods of time. This approach is called coerced abstinence.

As outlined by its major proponent, Mark A. R. Kleiman of the UCLA School of Public Policy and Social Research, coerced abstinence focuses on reduced drug consumption rather than on the intermediate goals of entry into treatment, retention, and compliance.[63] According to

Kleiman, a functional coerced abstinence program would do the following:

- screen probationers and parolees for drugs
- subject identified users to twice-weekly urine tests
- impose a brief, perhaps two-day, period of incarceration for every positive test
- impose sanctions immediately
- permit less frequent testing after a period, perhaps six months, of continuously clean tests

Of course, if some individuals are unable or unwilling to abstain under this pressure alone, it will be necessary to mandate treatment, with adverse consequences for failure. Yet, considering that only one-quarter of probationers report ever having been tested for drug use and that half the people who commit new crimes while on parole or probation are under the influence of drugs or alcohol, there can be little doubt that more consistent application of surveillance would yield benefits.[64]

The District of Columbia conducted an experiment in coerced abstinence as part of a drug demonstration project funded by the federal Center for Substance Abuse Treatment through the National Institute of Justice.[65] Between 1992 and 1995, the D.C. Pretrial Services Agency randomly assigned arrestees to three different presentencing tracks. In the "sanctions track," urine samples were obtained twice weekly, and arrestees were subject to increasingly severe penalties for missing or dirty urine samples. No formal treatment was provided, although individuals could seek it or could go voluntarily to Narcotics Anonymous.

The second treatment track was an intensive, daylong treatment program. The judge was kept informed about participants' performance but did not impose sanctions frequently or reliably. Finally, for the control group on the standard track, urine samples were collected twice a week, but there were no predictable consequences for missed or dirty samples.[66]

The Urban Institute analyzed the first 850 of 1,223 defendants to reach sentencing. The institute found that treatment-track participants were twice as likely to be drug-free in the month before sentencing as those in the standard track, by 27 percent versus 12 percent. But sanctions-track participants, subject to frequent urine testing and known consequences for violations, were three times as likely as standard-track participants to be drug-free during the same month, by 37 percent versus 12 percent. At six months after sentencing, rearrest rates for crimes of any kind were 2 percent for sanctions-track participants, 4 percent for the treatment track, and 6 percent for standard track participants.

Thus the researchers found that certainty of consequences was psychologically powerful. "The reason the sanctions-track people did so well," said senior researcher Adele Harrell, who conducted focus groups with study participants, "is because they knew what the judge would do. And he did it." Harrell also credited the "swiftness of the penalties—they had to report to court immediately for a test failure—and their fairness." One participant summed up to Harrell, "You get a dirty urine, man, you're going to jail. They're letting you know . . . you know the chances."

At least a dozen similar pilot programs and initiatives are in place, in cities in Arizona, California, Colorado, Connecticut, Michigan, and New York. Maryland's Break the Cycle program requires clinics to report to probation or parole officers within twenty-four hours after an addict has failed or skipped a drug test.[67] Project Sentry in Lansing, Michigan, in operation for twenty-five years, provides comparable testing, mostly short-term, for drug-involved offenders on probation or presentencing release. Offenders are tested three times a week, and drug use results in progressively more severe sanctions, beginning with three days in jail for the first positive or missed urine test, ten days for the second such failure, twenty for the third, and one month for each thereafter.

An evaluation of 5,000 participating offenders by the Michigan Office of Drug Control Policy found that 75 percent remained drug-free and were not arrested during the six-to-twelve–month observation period.[68]

In Coos County, Oregon, the number of positive results to probationers' drug tests has dropped since the adoption in 1988 of the Drug Reduction of Probationers program.[69] This program, too, is built around certain, swift responses to positive tests—immediate arrest and two days in jail for the first violation, ten days for the second, and thirty days for the third. Oregon officials found that prior to implementation of the program, 43 percent of all probationers tested positive for drugs. Within about six months after implementation, the figure was down to 10 percent.

Resistance to Coercion

Coercive strategies for drug treatment range from the least intrusive—social contracting, in which individuals are simply given incentives to behave in certain ways—to the most restrictive, such as forced treatment and confinement, in the face of life-threatening behavior. No matter where on this continuum a particular coercive strategy lies, however, it has met with significant resistance.

• One source of this resistance is the healthy reluctance we all feel to curtail anyone's personal autonomy. Political scientist James Q. Wilson has observed that this reluctance sometimes leads us to insist on the same freedom for others that we want for ourselves, even when the others in question have great difficulty in making use of such freedom.

• Many clinicians voice another objection to coercive strategies: they believe, mistakenly, that a patient must desire drug treatment in order to benefit from it.

• Another source of resistance is the current "medicalization" of addiction, the most recent round in the century-long debate over whether drug abuse should be treated on the medical model or the moral model.[70] Thus the National Institute on Drug Abuse of the National Institutes of Health now dubs addiction a "chronic and relapsing brain disease," as part of the institute's attempt to define addiction as simply another long-term medical condition like asthma or high blood pressure. This view, instead of challenging the inevitability of relapse by holding patients accountable for their choices, suggests the need for biological remedies for addiction. It also discounts the therapeutic potential of the coercion that the criminal justice system can exercise.[71]

Contrary to what this medicalized view would predict, however, the compulsion to take drugs does not necessarily dominate an addict's minute-to-minute or even day-to-day existence. The temporal architecture of his or her routine reveals that he is capable of reflection and purposeful behavior for some, perhaps a good deal, of the time. During the course of a heroin addict's day, for example, he may feel calm and his thoughts may be lucid as long as he is confident of access to drugs and he is using them in dosages adequate to prevent withdrawal but not large enough to be sedating. Likewise, there are periods in a cocaine addict's week when he is neither engaged in a binge nor wracked with intense craving for the drug. At these moments, he is not a victim controlled by brain disease. He might even choose to change his behavior—depending on what he thinks is at stake.[72]

This potential for self-control permits society to entertain and enforce expectations for addicts that would never be possible for someone who had, say, a brain tumor. Making such demands is of course no guarantee that they will be met. But confidence in the legitimacy of such demands would encourage a range of policy and therapeutic options, using consequences and coercion, that are incompatible with the idea of an exclusively no-fault brain disease.

• A final source of resistance to coercion in this therapeutic age is the belief that self-improvement is more successful and admirable when undertaken for one's self and one's self alone, not for anyone else or for the larger good. In this view, betterment achieved as a result of intrinsic motivation is more durable, and even more worthy, than is personal gain that is externally compelled.

But as we know, addicts are notoriously poor self-disciplinarians. They are also extremely ambivalent about giving up drugs, in spite of all the damage that drugs have caused them. Addicts' problems of self-governance demand that a rehabilitative regime for them include limit-setting, consistency, and sometimes physical containment.

Social Contracting. Contracting confers advantages on individuals when they manifest a desired behavior and penalizes them for violating expectations. For instance, addiction-impaired doctors, nurses, lawyers, and pilots may be allowed to keep their jobs or licenses "in exchange" for abstaining from illicit drugs or problem alcohol use under the close monitoring of a state professional society. Recall the public service announcement "Help an Addict: Threaten to Fire Him," made popular in the late 1980s by the Partnership for a Drug-Free America. Employers who follow that directive have established Employee Assistance Programs providing treatment for workers. With good effect, the military threatens drug- and alcohol-abusing soldiers with dishonorable discharges unless they abstain.

Most addicts admit being pressured into treatment by external forces such as health, employment, social relationships, financial conflicts, and emotional disturbances. Researchers estimate that only a small minority of addicts in treatment enrolled solely on personal initiative, unpressured by others.[73] Thus the therapeutic potential of contracting, for job security or other social opportunities, is considerable.

Employee assistance programs. These programs were first established as early as the 1940s by employers concerned about the effect of employee alcoholism on workplace safety and productivity. The Drug Free Workplace

Act of 1988 encouraged further expansion; currently, according to the Employee Assistance Professionals Association, there are some 20,000 EAPs nationwide. Four out of five Fortune 500 companies have one. From 20 to 60 percent of the EAP caseload is provided by mandatory referrals to treatment as an alternative to dismissal from work.[74]

Evidence suggests that individuals mandated to treatment through EAPs are as likely as voluntary participants, perhaps more likely, to profit from workplace-centered drug and alcohol treatment. In a study of industrial alcohol policy, Beaumont and Allsop found that workers mandated to treatment had better outcomes than had those who were self-referred.[75] The authors note that workers' age and length of service were positively correlated with both mandatory referral and improvement, interpreting these connections to mean that older workers felt a greater personal and professional investment in their jobs and thus responded more powerfully to the threat of job loss.

Walsh and colleagues conducted a randomized trial of treatment options for alcohol-abusing workers.[76] They assigned workers to one of three rehabilitation regimes: compulsory three-week inpatient treatment, compulsory attendance at Alcoholics Anonymous for a year, or a choice among options. During a two-year follow-up period, all groups showed comparable improvement in job performance. Individuals participating in the most restrictive option, however—inpatient treatment—were significantly less likely than the others to relapse.

Researchers at the University of Pennsylvania made a similar study of 304 transportation and city service union members in Philadelphia.[77] One group, of 111 individuals, was referred to the union's EAP because of positive urine tests during random screening at the worksite; another group of 103 was self-referred. For the first, coerced, group, failure to abide by the terms of the evaluation and referral procedures was grounds for dismissal. Although most of these coerced individuals were "resistant to entering any treatment setting," all attended treatment. The level of verification in the study was high: there were urine tests, self-reports of earnings were checked against pay stubs, and self-reported criminal convictions were checked against arrest records.

The researchers found that coerced individuals were more likely to complete a course of treatment than were self-referred workers. Seventy-seven percent of the coerced workers in inpatient care and 74 percent of coerced workers in outpatient counseling finished. Comparable figures for voluntary workers were 61 percent and 60 percent, respectively. At a six-month follow-up, 92 percent of all participating workers were reinterviewed; coerced and voluntary patients showed similar levels of improvement. "This is interesting," the authors note, "in that many clinicians feel strongly that intrinsic motivation is a prerequisite for engagement and improvement. . . . [F]or the participants in the study, the coercive referral condition did not hinder the chances for successful treatment."

The American Civil Liberties Union, however, has condemned the workplace drug testing that serves as an element of this strategy. "Employers need to kick the drug test habit," said ACLU legislative counsel Solange Bitol in testimony before the House Small Business Subcommittee on Empowerment on a proposal to provide $10 million to small businesses for drug testing. The ACLU objected not merely to using taxpayer money for this purpose but to the activity of employer testing per se.

Public agencies. Increasingly, public agencies are fighting to adopt a quid pro quo strategy toward drug abuse. In 1996 a federal judge ruled in favor of the New York City Housing Authority's efforts to obtain expedited court-ordered evictions in cases involving drugs and other threatening behavior. Previously, such evictions had taken two years or more to carry out. The Legal Aid Society of New York City argued against the new eviction procedure, filing court papers on behalf of tenants (without ever having consulted one), despite overwhelming tenant support for the Housing Authority's plan.[78]

In Dallas, Alphonso Jackson, president of the city's Housing Authority from 1989 to 1996, asked tenants to agree to undergo drug testing as a condition of living in the special Self-Sufficiency Program within Dallas public housing. He was made a defendant in numerous lawsuits on the issue filed by the ACLU and legal aid organizations.[79]

The Doe Foundation in New York City, which operates the Ready, Willing, and Able training program, became the target of a similar lawsuit after it took over a Harlem men's shelter in 1996. The shelter, at the time of the takeover, was described as a "lawless crack den."[80] The foundation reports that it began requiring applicants to the shelter to be drug-free as a condition of acceptance and, once enrolled as trainees, to be drug tested routinely. In addition, the foundation required that residents work in street-cleaning and house-painting operations. Initially, 62 percent of the residents tested positive in scheduled, pre-announced tests. Nine months later, they report, only 2 percent were testing positive in random tests.

In 1997, the Coalition for the Homeless and Legal Aid sued the foundation. What raised these advocates' ire was the requirement that residents work as a condition of participation. Even though the programs pay each participant, the coalition denounced them as "tools for slave masters."

These plaintiffs could look for a precedent to a 1995 trial court opinion by Justice Helen Freedman in Manhattan.[81] She ruled that residents of public family shelters could not be obligated to follow rules and regulations such as drug testing, curfews, and job training.

The fight over drug testing has engaged other public bodies as well. The ACLU has fought efforts by public high schools to perform random drug tests on students, even those who would first require consent from parents. This controversy went all the way to the Supreme Court, which ruled such policies constitutionally permissible.[82]

Despite the challenges, many not-for-profit homeless shelters and churches require abstinence as a condition of receiving services. As we have seen, there is even a state-funded methadone clinic, in Baltimore, that requires patients to be employed and drug-free as a condition of remaining in the program.

Courts, too, are experimenting with various forms of social contracting. Over the years, judges have noted that a high percentage of child abuse and neglect cases involve substance abuse by parents; a fact sheet issued by the National Committee to Prevent Child Abuse puts the figure at up to 80 percent.[83] Accordingly, a few cities—Pensacola, Florida; Kalamazoo, Michigan; Kansas City, Missouri; Reno, Nevada; and New York City—have recently established Family Drug Courts. Though little information is as yet available on outcomes, these new institutions are notable because they are determined to use incentives such as child custody, visitation privileges, and the removal of children from homes as leverage to compel parents to comply with drug treatment and remain drug-free.

Welfare reform legislation, too, has stimulated many states and localities to revise their procedures for awarding benefits. For example, Montgomery County, Maryland, now denies benefits to applicants who refuse to undergo drug testing.

With estimates of problem substance abuse among welfare recipients estimated to be between 15 and 30 percent (although, according to the Legal Action Center, some states put the figure as high as 50 percent), the efficiency of surveillance and sanctioning procedures will be put to the test.[84] Although social service organizations do not yet capitalize on their built-in potential for leverage, more will be doing so as the public demands more civic responsibility from beneficiaries.

Contingency Management. The goal of this technique (CM) is to intervene in an addict's life with an arrangement of environmental consequences—rewards, punishments, or both—to weaken drug use systematically and strengthen the skills necessary for abstinence. The underlying behavioral theory, operant conditioning, holds that the act of using drugs can be modified by its consequences.

The earliest CM studies were conducted with alcoholics. Miller and colleagues, for example, examined the question of whether CM could be used to reduce public drunkenness.[85] They selected twenty alcoholic men from the city jail in Jackson, Mississippi, and randomly assigned them to an experimental or control group. Men in the experimental group, if they reduced their drinking, could earn housing, employment, food, and medical care from cooperating local social service agencies. Men in the control group, by contrast, received these services whether they were drunk or sober. The researchers assessed the men's alcohol intake objectively, by breath alcohol levels or observation of gross intoxication.

Over the course of the two-month study, arrests in the experimental group decreased by 85 percent. In the control group, they did not decline at all.

In the past decade, researchers have begun studying CM in depth. Although sample sizes tend to be small and follow-up limited in duration, the findings are so consistently promising that CM merits close review. Stephen Higgins and colleagues at the University of Vermont have produced a detailed summary of CM studies involving abusers of heroin and cocaine;[86] a few representative studies are described below.

Higgins and his colleagues conducted numerous CM trials with cocaine addicts.[87] In a 1994 study, forty patients were randomly assigned to either ordinary treatment or treatment plus vouchers. The vouchers, assigned a monetary value and exchangeable for retail items, were awarded on a schedule of increasing value with each consecutive clean urine sample submitted; conversely, a cocaine-positive sample would reset the value of the vouchers at their initial low level.

At the end of twenty-four weeks, 75 percent of the voucher group remained active, compared with only 40 percent of the nonvoucher group. For the voucher group, the average duration of continuous cocaine abstinence, documented by urine tests, was twelve weeks; for the nonvoucher group it was six weeks. At nine and twelve months after entry into the study, self-reported cocaine use remained significantly lower in the voucher group.

A similar study took place in Baltimore, conducted by Ken Silverman and colleagues at Johns Hopkins University and involving thirty-seven inner-city methadone-maintenance patients who concurrently abused cocaine.[88] During the twelve-week study, all patients received standard counseling. A group of nineteen received vouchers contingent on cocaine-negative urine tests, while eighteen received vouchers on a schedule linked to that of the experimental group but dispensed independently of urine test results. The parallel dispensing of vouchers to the two groups was meant to uncouple the effects of voucher receipt itself from its meaning as a reward predictably dependent on urine test results.

At the end of the three-month study, the experimental group had substantially reduced cocaine usage, but the comparison group remained largely unchanged. About half the patients exposed to the contingent vouchers had achieved between seven and twelve weeks of continuous abstinence; by contrast, fewer than 5 percent of the control group had attained as many as three consecutive weeks of abstinence.

Although there was a rebound resumption of drug use after the contingent vouchers were discontinued, as in most other CM studies, the experimental group performed significantly better at all stages of follow-up.

Intensified CM techniques have had results even for subgroups resistant to voucher incentives. To examine such populations, Silverman and his colleagues chose a sample of intravenous cocaine-abusing patients, many of them also HIV-positive, who had failed a standard CM voucher experiment.[89] The researchers ran these individuals, in randomized order, through three different nine-week voucher regimes: one in which the total redeemable value of vouchers that could be earned was high, one in which it was low, and one in which it was zero.

The findings were dramatic. Not a single patient in the zero-value voucher program achieved more than two weeks of abstinence. Only one person did so in the low-value program. But in the high-value voucher program, 45 percent attained at least four weeks of sustained abstinence.[90]

The major drawback of these CM studies—patients' tendency to resume drug use, albeit at a lower level, when the contract is withdrawn—also reveals the major potential of CM for entitlement reform. The backsliding of patients in the studies was probably attributable in part to the short duration of these research projects: a mere few months is not enough time to enable a patient to learn the new skills, secure the employment, and attain the measure of personal growth needed to live drug-free. Entitlement reform need not be limited by such constraints.

Contingency Management under Real-World Conditions. Jesse Milby of the University of Alabama sought to apply CM in a situation that approximated real-world conditions.[91] He randomized 176 homeless, crack-addicted individuals to receive ordinary or enhanced care. Members of the enhanced group, after two months of daily intensive therapy, were eligible to participate in a work-therapy program refurbishing condemned housing and, for a modest rental fee, to live in this housing. Participation was contingent on submitting twice-weekly clean urine tests.

After six months, this group had achieved significantly greater improvement in employment status, days of homelessness, and cocaine use than had the usual-care group.

At Seattle's Harborview Medical Center, psychiatrist

Richard K. Reis directs a clinic for mentally ill substance abusers.[92] Clinic patients are asked to sign over their Supplemental Security Income checks to the outpatient clinic, which then acts as the patients' "representative payee," managing bank accounts on their behalf. The clinic covers rent and other basics. By complying with treatment, patients are allowed to "earn back" discretionary funds and ultimately, when they demonstrate ability to manage money responsibly, to control the passbooks to their bank accounts.

Ries and his colleagues compared treatment outcomes between patients in the incentive program and those attending the clinic as usual. Over a three-month period, sicker patients were significantly more likely than their healthier counterparts to attend treatment sessions and were just as likely to participate in job training sessions and stay out of the hospital and jail.

Studies such as these suggest that with drug-abusing individuals, manipulating benefits to reinforce positive social behavior could provide a partial solution to the perverse incentives that entitlements often provide. Street ethnographers have long known that addicts routinely purchase drugs with welfare payments and food stamps; more recent quantitative reports have described a persistent temporal pattern in which receipt of monthly benefits is linked to increases in emergency-room visits for intoxication and overdoses, and in hospitalizations for psychosis among cocaine-abusing schizophrenics.

Thus the Veterans Administration has instituted a CM project that would distribute veterans' service-connected benefits contingently to mentally ill substance abusers.[93] Conceivably, federal disability payments, welfare benefits, and other forms of cash entitlement could be dispensed in accordance with CM principles.

Coercion of Pregnant Addicts. The clash between the need for coercion and resistance to coercive strategies has been especially marked when the subjects have been drug-addicted pregnant women. Pregnant women have in fact been subjects of CM trials. Using incentives such as goods-redeemable vouchers or baby supplies donated by neighborhood businesses, researchers have succeeded in increasing attendance at prenatal clinics while reducing drug use.

The criminal justice system has embarked on even more coercive strategies for pregnant addicts, arousing intense controversy in the process.[94] Prosecutors in many states have gone so far as to bring criminal charges against pregnant women who abuse drugs. Some prosecutors have used child-endangerment statutes; others have charged delivery of drugs to a minor (via the umbilical cord). The reasonable assumption has been that a pregnant woman who cannot bring herself to stop abusing drugs or alcohol—either directly, or through self-imposed "cold turkey" withdrawal, or through treatment—is either so profoundly physiologically addicted that she is not competent to protect her unborn child or, if not physiologically addicted, so irresponsible as to be unfit for unsupervised parenthood. The primary goal of bringing charges, accordingly, has been to protect the baby by coercing the woman into residential treatment as an alternative to trial or incarceration.

The most publicized cases of such coercion occurred in Charleston, South Carolina. Staff at the Medical University of South Carolina became concerned about the increasing numbers of cocaine-related complications of late-term pregnancy. Nurses and doctors tried unsuccessfully to convince women at risk to enter drug treatment.

In 1989, the hospital adopted a policy of required urine screening if a woman met any of several criteria: no prenatal care, detached placenta, stillbirth, preterm labor, intrauterine growth retardation, or mother's previously known drug or alcohol abuse. Of women who screened positive, none kept her assigned appointment at the medical center's substance abuse clinic. When these women returned to the hospital in preterm labor, their urine screens were again uniformly positive. After delivery, each woman again refused an appointment for drug treatment.[95]

In late 1989, the Charleston Police Department and the state's Office of the Solicitor became involved, and policy became more restrictive. Any woman testing positive who refused an appointment with the substance abuse or prenatal clinic was arrested and charged with either possession of an illegal drug or, if her urine or her infant's drug test was positive at the time of delivery, distribution of drugs to a minor. In early 1990, the policy was modified to allow a woman to avoid arrest by successfully completing treatment. Women who declined such treatment were placed on probation.

A report on the operation of this policy, published in the *Journal of the South Carolina Medical Association*, indicates that the incidence of positive urine screens for cocaine dropped dramatically after the restrictive policy was implemented, from more than twenty per month to five or six per month.[96]

Authors of the report acknowledged that the program was controversial. "Critics of our protocol," they wrote, "point out that the threat of legal problems may have driven obstetric patients away." They noted, though, that "delivery rates remained constant, and the Medical University remains the only facility within a 50 mile radius which offers obstetric care for indigent and Medicaid patients. Consequently it is unlikely that these patients could have delivered at neighboring facilities." Nor did the number of home births increase during the year after the policy went into effect.

The South Carolina experience suggests that mandatory treatment of pregnant addicts who have previously rejected voluntary treatment leads to the birth of healthier babies and does not deter women from giving birth in hospitals. Nevertheless, the issue has galvanized women's advocacy groups.[97] The Center for Reproductive Law and Policy, condemning the South Carolina program as an excuse to "punish women for their behavior during pregnancy," is pursuing a lawsuit against the state.

This suit is a continuation of a campaign against the Medical University of South Carolina that began in 1992, when the Office of Civil Rights in the U.S. Department of Health and Human Services (HHS) sent investigators to the hospital to determine whether racial discrimination had occurred. The next year, the Center for Reproductive Law and Policy filed a civil action against the medical center, also alleging racial discrimination. In 1997, U.S. District Judge C. Weston Houck ruled that there was no basis for the charge. "The catalyst for targeting these individuals [African-American plaintiffs] was a policy designed to prevent cocaine abuse in pregnant women," the judge wrote, opining that "plaintiffs have not shown a statistically significant disparate impact on black women in this case."

The medical center, despite its legal victory, discontinued its carrot-and-stick policy in 1994 in response to a threat by HHS to cut the hospital's federal funding.

Civil Commitment. Perhaps the greatest controversy about coercive strategies has arisen over the issue of civil commitment. When an addict has sustained significant temporary brain damage from compulsive drug taking, then this ultimate intrusion is warranted.[98] Such time-limited, often life-saving suspension of autonomy allows for urgent medical attention to suicidal impulses, severe depression, or psychosis.

More than half the states now have statutes that allow judges to commit an addicted person to treatment without his or her consent in much the same way that they can mandate a gravely disabled mentally ill person to undergo treatment in a psychiatric hospital.[99] The process is appropriate for addicted individuals considered incompetent to attend to their own welfare and safety; the standard for this form of coercion is helplessness, not necessarily dangerousness to society.

As early as 1870, the American Association for the Cure of Inebriety tried to persuade states to create institutions in which doctors could treat and confine alcoholics and drug "habitues" rather than send them to jail. In the 1930s, narcotics farms were able, in a similar way, to accommodate some so-called civil addicts whose severe addiction made them dysfunctional but who were not involved in crime.

As we have seen, California and New York used civil commitment extensively in the 1960s and 1970s. Unsurprisingly, the constitutionality of the process has been challenged; but the Supreme Court has upheld the process. Since then, the California Supreme Court and the New York State Court of Appeals have also upheld civil commitment, reasoning that life-threatening developments—the college student so heavily addicted to cocaine that she drops out of school to work as a prostitute in a crack house, or the homeless addict who refuses to see a doctor for a gangrenous foot—can justify the intrusion into personal autonomy.[100]

Nevertheless, civil commitment of addicts now occurs only occasionally, usually when a desperate loved one or concerned physician brings an addicted individual to the attention of a judge.

Conclusion

Coercion has been applied in the service of rehabilitating addicts for more than seventy years. The experience has yielded a powerful clinical lesson: Addicts need not be internally motivated at the outset of treatment in order to benefit from it. Indeed, addicts who are legally pressured into treatment may outperform voluntary patients, because they are likely to stay in treatment longer and are more likely to graduate. Without formal coercive mechanisms, the treatment system would not attract many of the most dysfunctional addicts, and surely could not retain them.

But although official bodies—especially criminal justice organizations—are accustomed to wielding such leverage, they do not do so systematically enough to yield maximum benefit.[101] Some judges will forgo referral to treatment altogether if they perceive an offender not to be motivated toward rehabilitation.[102] Other judges express disappointment with the laxity of supervision addicts receive in treatment, citing failure to follow up with the court, verify patient participation, and perform drug testing—the very surveillance mechanisms that are necessary to retain unmotivated addicts.

Ironically, it appears that among current programs, with their various mixtures of treatment and coercion, the treatment component has relatively less clout than other forces have in shaping addicts' behavior. That is why examples of combining treatment with external monitoring, as in employee assistance programs and drug courts, are so encouraging. If more institutions, including public housing or even disability programs, adopted principles of contingency management, individuals would be likely to remain in treatment longer and enjoy greater improvement. Such behavioral gains would serve both addicts and the communities whose resources they strain.

A coordinated effort by social service agencies to track and monitor drug use and to enforce consequences for that use will be costly in the short run. In addition, it will require the creation of a certain amount of new bureaucracy. Those facts make coercive strategies unattractive even to those who are sympathetic to the need for aggressive intervention. It remains true, however, that as a clinical strategy, coercion is solidly promising. What is more, increasing our capacity to leverage addicts into treatment will be important whether we maintain our present policy of drug prohibition, decide on a policy of outright legalization, or choose anything in between, since any one of these policies will depend on drug treatment to rehabilitate addicts.

Addiction impairs participation in a free society. It interferes with the ability to ensure one's own welfare, respect the safety of others, and discharge responsibilities as a parent, spouse, worker, neighbor, or citizen. Addiction is a behavioral condition for which the prescription of choice is the imposition of reliable consequences and rewards, often combined with coercion that keeps the addicted individual from fleeing treatment. To say this is not punitive; it is clinically sound and empirically justified.

Every day, all people respond to contingencies, incentives, and consequences. If we do not work, we do not get paid. If rent is not paid, we are evicted. If children are mistreated, they can be taken away. Meeting obligations in these circumstances is not the antithesis of freedom but a prerequisite to it. No less is this true of individuals with drug problems, though it is our job to structure the contingencies before them in creative ways to help them regain their freedom.

Notes

1. The Office of National Drug Control Policy (ONDCP), Executive Office of the President, defines *treatment gap* as the difference between the number of people needing treatment and the number receiving it. Based on data from the National Household Survey on Drug Abuse, the gap in 1994 was 1.7 million people: an estimated 3,553,000 needed treatment and 1,847,000 received it. Information from the Uniform Crime Report and the Uniform Facility Data Set are also used to calculate the gap. (From personal communication with Janie B. Dargan, Office of Planning, Budget, and Research, May 29, 1998.)

Typically, six to eight years elapse between initiation of problem use and first treatment, according to the Drug Abuse Treatment Outcome Study (DATOS). (See *Psychology of Addictive Behaviors*, entire December 1997 issue, vol. 11.) The shorter the period of dysfunction, the better the chance of regaining social and personal competence.

2. Definitional and methodological issues abound. The term *coerced treatment* has been used interchangeably with *compulsory treatment*, *mandated treatment*, *involuntary treatment*, *legal pressure into treatment*, and *criminal justice referral to treatment*. See M. D. Anglin, M. L. Prendergast, and D. Farabee, "The Effectiveness of Coerced Treatment for Drug Abusing Offenders," presented at the Office of National Drug Control Policy's Conference of Scholars and Policy Makers, Washington, D.C., March 25, 1998. (Paper available on ONDCP website <www.whitehousedrugpolicy.gov>.) Researcher George DeLeon considered separately the often interchangeable terms *legal status, legal referral, and legal*

pressure. Legal status, he noted, means any form of legal involvement, including being arrested, in jail, awaiting trial, or out on bail. Legal referral indicates any one of a variety of criminal justice procedures that direct addicts to a treatment alternative, such as pretrial rehabilitation services, parole, probation, or sentencing stipulations. Legal pressure, however, refers to the individual's perception of the forces impinging on him. In one analysis, it appeared that retention depended more on the mere presence of criminal justice pressure than on its level of intensity. (See M. L. Hiller, K. Knight, K. M. Broome, and D. D. Simpson, "Legal Pressure and Treatment Retention in a National Sample of Long-Term Residential Program," *Criminal Justice and Behavior,* vol. 25, 1998, pp. 463–81.)

Differences in the personal meaning of coercion have prompted evaluators to consider a more subtle analysis of "treatment under pressure." After all, not every formally coerced addict is a resistant one. Indeed, approximately one-half of inmates surveyed in a Texas prison said they would be willing to participate in treatment—even if it meant remaining incarcerated for three additional months. See D. Farabee, *Substance Abuse among Male Inmates Entering the Texas Department of Criminal Justice-Institutional Division* (Austin, Texas: Texas Commission on Alcohol and Drug Abuse, 1993). Yet 25 to 35 percent of incarcerated offenders still refuse the option of treatment and prefer jail time, dispelling the popular belief that drug treatment "coddles" addicts. See D. L. MacKenzie and C. Sourya, *Multisite Evaluation of Shock Incarceration* (Washington, D.C.: National Institute of Mental Health, 1994); J. Petersilia and S. Turner, "Evaluating Intensive Supervision Probation/Parole: Results of a Nationwide Experiment" (Washington, D.C.: National Institute of Justice, 1993); Report to ONDCP, "Reducing Recidivism through a Seamless System of Care: Components of Effective Treatment, Supervision and Transition Services in the Community," February 20, 1998. According to criminologist Faye Taxman at the University of Maryland, author of the February 20, 1998, report, some defense attorneys consider treatment programs "a risk for their clients because failure to comply may result in more incarceration time [than otherwise imposed]."

But what about addict-offenders who are not given the option of refusing treatment? Douglas Young and colleagues at the Vera Institute for Justice explored this question. They devised a construct called Perceived Legal Pressure (PLP) and applied the measure to a modest-sized group of drug felons in mandatory residential treatment. The PLP index measured respondents' views that (a) conditions of the treatment mandate would be enforced, (b) their behavior would be closely monitored, and (c) the consequences for failing treatment would be severe. After controlling for other clinical characteristics, the researchers found that retention correlated with the perception that monitors were vigilant and that absconding from the program agents would result in certain and immediate apprehension. Notably, the perceived aversion to prison was only marginally associated with higher retention. (See D. Young, P. Dynia, and S. Belenko, "How Compelling Is Coerced Treatment: A Study of Different Mandated Approaches," presented at the annual meeting of the American Society of Criminology, Chicago, November 22, 1996.)

3. J. Jonnes, *Hep-Cats, Narcs, and Pipe Dreams: A History of America's Romance with Illegal Drugs* (New York: Scribner, 1996).

4. D. F. Musto, *The American Disease: Origins of Narcotic Control* (2nd ed.) (New York: Oxford University Press, 1987); also, W. L. White, *Slaying the Dragon: The History of Addiction Treatment and Recovery in America* (Bloomington, Illinois: Chestnut Health Services/Lighthouse Institute, 1998), chapter 13.

5. Jonnes, *Hep-Cats*, p. 55.

6. J. A. Inciardi, "Some Considerations on the Clinical Efficacy of Compulsory Treatment: Reviewing the New York Experience," in C. G. Leukefeld and F. M. Tims, eds., *Compulsory Treatment of Drug Abuse: Research and Clinical Practice* (Washington, D.C.: U.S. Government Printing Office, 1988), NIDA Research Monograph 86, DHHS Publication No. ADM 89-1578.

7. Jonnes, *Hep-Cats*, pp. 111–12.

8. U.S. Comptroller General, *Limited Use of Federal Programs to Commit Narcotics Addicts for Treatment and Rehabilitation*, September 20, 1971.

9. M. J. Pescor, *Public Health Report* (Supplement) 170, 1943, follow-up study of treated narcotics addicts. For more discussion, see Leukefeld and Tims, *Compulsory Treatment of Drug Abuse*.

10. G. E. Vaillant, "The Role of Compulsory Supervision in the Treatment of Addiction," *Federal Probation,* vol. 30, 1966, pp. 53–59.

11. G. De Leon, "Legal Pressure in Therapeutic Communities," in Leukefeld and Tims, *Compulsory Treatment of Drug Abuse*. Although he has studied this process most extensively among patients treated in residential programs—self-contained, live-in "therapeutic communities" lasting one to two years—De Leon's scheme likely operates in any compulsory treatment setting. G. De Leon, G. Melnick, and D. Kressel, "Motivation and Readiness for Therapeutic Community Treatment among Cocaine and Other Drug Abusers," *American Journal of Drug and Alcohol Abuse*, vol. 23, 1997, pp. 169–89.

What can we expect from treatment? The major studies show that patient drug use and criminal activity are markedly reduced during treatment itself. Upon completion, between one-third and one-half of patients are able to remain abstinent from their "drug of choice" one year later. (See M. L. Prendergast, Y. I. Hser, J. Chen, and J. Hsieh, "Drug Treatment Need among Offender Populations," paper presented at the 44th Annual Meeting of the American Society of Criminology, New Orleans, Louisiana, November 4–7, 1992.) Since few patients complete programs, however, enduring abstinence is a rare result of treatment. Nevertheless, considerable reductions in drug use and crime are consistently demonstrated.

In the Drug Abuse Reporting Project (DARP), daily use of heroin was down by an average of 60 percent one year after treatment, irrespective of modality, ranging from 64 percent among methadone patients to 56 percent among outpatient clinic patients. Employment increased two- to three-fold at one year, and incarceration declined by one-half to two-thirds, relative to pretreatment levels. Within the subset of patients followed for twelve years, 63 percent had been drug-free for three years. This is almost twice the rate of developmental "maturing out" (or, retirement from a lifelong career of addiction) that one expects to see among a cohort of aging heroin users. Unless a patient stayed beyond a threshold treatment stay of three months, however, his status one year after treatment would be unchanged from pretreatment levels.

Among Treatment Outcome Prospective Study (TOPS) patients, daily cocaine and heroin rates were down by about half at one year after treatment, as long as the length of stay exceeded three months. But the most impressive reductions were seen among those who stayed at least one year. Patients who remained for at least three months dropped at-least weekly use of cocaine by one-third to two-thirds by the fifth year. Regular heroin use declined between 50 percent and 75 percent by the fifth year. Predatory crime declined by one-third to one-half, while employment doubled among those in outpatient and residential programs; it declined for those on methadone. Unfortunately, however, use of alcohol and marijuana increased. Similarly, DATOS patients at one-year follow-up cut both weekly and daily usage of cocaine and heroin by one-half, if they stayed for at least three to six months.

12. G. De Leon, H. K. Wexler, and N. Jainchill, "The Therapeutic Community: Success and Improvement Rates Five Years after Treatment," *The International Journal of Addictions,* vol.17, no. 4, 1982, pp. 703– 47.

13. Leukefeld and Tims, *Compulsory Treatment of Drug Abuse.* See also M. D. Anglin and Y. Hser, "Legal Coercion and Drug Abuse Treatment: Research Findings and Social Policy Implications," in J. A. Inciardi, ed., *Handbook of Drug Control in the United States* (New York: Greenwood Press, 1990); and Hiller, Knight, Broome, and Simpson, "Legal Pressure and Treatment Retention." A recent analysis from a large treatment sample (DATOS) suggests that retention may depend more on the mere presence of the criminal justice pres-

sure than on the level of its intensity and the risk of incarceration; see M. D. Anglin, M. L. Prendergast, and D. Farabee, "The Effectiveness of Coerced Treatment for Drug Abusing Offenders," presented at the Office of National Drug Control Policy's Conference of Scholars and Policy Makers, Washington, D.C., March 25, 1998. (This paper is available on ONDCP site <www.whitehousedrugpolicy.gov>.) In the paper, Douglas Anglin and colleagues at the Drug Abuse Research Center at UCLA explicitly took differing terminology into account in their review of studies of coerced treatment. They concluded that "legally referred clients do as well or better than voluntary clients in and after treatment . . . and [since] controlling drug abuse and addiction benefits society as a whole, the criminal justice system should bring drug-abusing offenders into treatment as a safeguard and [so] promote the interests and well-being of the community." See also D. B. Marlowe, D. J. Glass, E. P. Merikle, D. S. Festinger, D. S. DeMatteo, G. R. Marczyk, and J. J. Platt, "Efficacy of Coercion in Substance Abuse Treatment," in F. Tims, C. Leukefeld, and J. J. Platt, eds., *Relapse and Recovery in the Addictions* (New Haven, Connecticut: Yale University Press, forthcoming); and J. Langenbucher, B. S. McCrady, J. Brick, and R. Esterly, *Socioeconomic Evaluations of Addictions Treatment* (Washington, D.C.: White House Printing Office, 1993).

14. D. B. Marlowe, K. C. Kirby, L. M. Bonieskie, D. J. Glass, L. D. Dodds, S. D. Husband, J. J. Platt, and D. S. Festinger, "Assessment of Coercive and Noncoercive Pressures to Enter Drug Abuse Treatment," *Drug and Alcohol Dependence,* vol. 42, 1996, pp. 77–84.

15. De Leon, Wexler, and Jainchill, "The Therapeutic Community."

16. Leukefeld and Tims, *Compulsory Treatment of Drug Abuse.* According to Drug Abuse Treatment Outcome Study, patients most likely to stay in treatment are those with: high motivation; legal pressure; no prior trouble with the law; psychological counseling while in treatment; and lack of other psychological problems, especially antisocial personality disorder.

17. G. De Leon, "Legal Pressure in Therapeutic Communities."

18. D. F. Musto, *The American Disease,* and W. L. White, *Slaying the Dragon.*

19. J. H. Lowinson, I. J. Marion, H. Joseph, and V. P. Dole, "Methadone Maintenance," in J. H. Lowinson, P. Ruiz, and R. B. Millman, eds., *Substance Abuse Treatment: A Comprehensive Textbook,* 2nd ed. (Baltimore, Maryland: Williams and Wilkins, 1992).

20. M. D. Anglin, "The Efficacy of Civil Commitment in Treating Narcotic Addiction," in Leukefeld and Tims, *Compulsory Treatment of Drug Abuse*; Anglin, "Efficacy of Civil Commitment in Treating Narcotics Addiction," *Journal of Drug Issues,* vol.18, 1988, pp. 527– 45.

21. M. Kidorf, J. R. Hollander, V. L. King, and R. K. Brooner, "Increasing Employment of Opioid Dependent Outpatients: An Intensive Behavioral Intervention," *Drug and Alcohol Dependence,* vol. 50, 1998, pp.73–80.

22. W. H. McGlothlin, M. D. Anglin, and B. D. Wilson, *An Evaluation of the California Civil Addict Program*, DHEW pub. no. (ADM) 78-558, National Institute on Drug Abuse, 1977. According to Anglin, the CAP program changed dramatically after the advent of determinant sentencing in California in the 1970s. After determinant sentencing, it was possible for the required stay in CAP to be longer than the incarceration period, a condition that mitigated against the offender choosing treatment. Treatment at the main in-custody facility, the California Rehabilitation Center in Corona, now consists primarily of drug education efforts. Currently, the state legislature is considering a bill to revitalize the CAP and return the services provided to a level reminiscent of its initial decade. (Personal communication, July 1, 1998.)

23. Annual address, Message to the Legislature, State of New York, January 3, 1973.

24. J. H. Jaffe, "The Swinging Pendulum: The Treatment of Drug Users in America," in R. DuPont, R. Goldstein, and S. O'Donnell, eds., *Handbook on Drug Abuse* (Washington, D.C.: U.S. Government Printing Office, 1979).

25. D. D. Simpson, S. B. Sells, "Effectiveness of Treatment

for Drug Abuse: An Overview of the DARP Research Program," *Advances in Alcohol and Substance Abuse*, vol. 2, 1983, pp. 7–29; R. L. Hubbard, M. E. Marsden, J. V. Rachal, J. H. Harwood, E. R. Cavanaugh, and H. M. Ginzburg, *Drug Abuse Treatment: A National Study of Effectiveness* (Chapel Hill, North Carolina: University of North Carolina Press, 1989); D. D. Simpson, S. J. Curry, eds., "Special Issue: Drug Abuse Treatment Outcome Study," *Psychology of Addictive Behaviors*, vol. 11; Center for Substance Abuse Treatment, *National Treatment Improvement Evaluation Study, Preliminary Report: Persistent Effects of Substance Abuse Treatment—One Year Later*, September 1996.

DARP, TOPS, and DATOS were funded by the National Institute on Drug Abuse of the National Institutes of Health. The National Treatment Improvement Evaluation Study (NTIES) was funded by the Center for Substance Abuse Treatment of the Substance Abuse and Mental Health Services Administration.

In March 1997, the Substance Abuse and Mental Health Services Administration completed a congressionally mandated study of the treatment facilities it supports. The NTIES followed about 4,400 patients treated in seventy-eight representative facilities. Eighty-two percent of enrolled patients were followed for one year after leaving treatment. A relatively large portion, 36 percent, actually completed treatment, but the threshold for defining completion was low (under one year). The average length of stay was fourteen weeks, and only 13 percent stayed for more than six months. In a subset of patients, self-reported data were validated with urine tests and review of arrest records. Drug use was reduced by roughly half at one year, and arrests went down by 63 percent. Outcomes for the 38 percent who were legally pressured (defined as having treatment "required or recommended" by court, prison, or probation or parole officer) were similar to outcomes for voluntary patients. Pressured patients remained in treatment slightly longer and were more likely to complete it.

Caution is warranted in interpreting treatment outcome studies. Among the hundreds of studies on treatment outcome, only a modest number have overcome the following methodological challenges:

• *Lack of random assignment.* Randomization of control-and-comparison groups eliminates the confounding problem of self-selection, which can be influenced by patient preference, perception of treatment type, and treatment availability. It is rarely done, however, in large-scale, long-term studies of substance abuse treatment. Practical difficulties aside, one reason is that researchers assume random assignment would require an enormous sample to compensate for dropouts. These dropouts are anticipated to result from the assignment of patients to the "wrong" treatment modality. Consequently, effectiveness studies typically employ a pretreatment vs. posttreatment comparison design in which patients serve as their own controls. Another option is to compare addicts waiting to get into treatment with those already enrolled; this avoids the ethical problems associated with assigning individuals to a placebo (no treatment) group.

• *Reliance on self-reported measures of drug use and crime.* The reliability of self-reporting is highly variable. On the one hand, study participants have a variety of obvious reasons to misrepresent their drug use and criminal involvement, making data collected from criminal populations problematic. On the other hand, some studies, such as DARP, the largest outcome analysis ever undertaken, found good agreement between drug tests and self-report. E. D. Wish and his colleagues examined the relationship between self-reported drug use and urinalysis results to rearrest figures in a sample of 1,180 people arrested in Washington, D.C., in 1989. E. D. Wish, J. A. Hoffman, and S. Nemes, "The Validity of Self-Reports of Drug Use at Treatment Admission and at Follow-Up: Comparisons with Urinalysis and Hair Analysis," in L. Harrison and A. Hughes, eds., *The Validity of Self-Reported Drug Use: Improving the Accuracy of Survey Estimates,* NIDA Research Monograph 167, Rockville, Maryland, 1997. Only 31 percent reported using cocaine in the twenty-four to seventy-two hours preceding arrest, while double that proportion, 63 percent of the sample, had a positive urine test.

Furthermore, accuracy of self-report may also vary according to the type of drug abused and whether the data were solicited before or after treatment. Alternatively, the NTIES study found that self-report of use of crack and cocaine since treatment was actually higher than revealed by urine testing. This suggests that some short-acting substances are "missed" by testing and that the subset of large-trial subjects who explicitly agreed to be tested may be especially forthcoming in reporting their behavior.

The recent review published by the National Institute on Drug Abuse (see above) emphasizes the limitations of self-reported data. In general, data show, self-reports are less valid for the more stigmatized drugs, such as crack and heroin; for more recent use than for past use; and for those involved in the criminal justice system. Then again, patients may over-report drug use to make their problem seem worse and thus expedite their admission into treatment, or for fear of impending withdrawal. The use of toxicology screening (such as urine, hair, or blood) largely circumvents the limitations of self-report, just as reliance on documented police or criminal justice records is the gold standard for quantifying criminal activity; but verification on a large scale often imposes an unacceptable burden on the researchers' resources. Indeed, a 1998 report from the General Accounting Office, entitled *Research Shows Treatment Is Effective, but Benefits May Be Overstated*, cited legitimate concern about the validity of self-report. See General Accounting Office, *Drug Abuse: Research Shows Treatment Is Effective, but Benefits May Be Overstated*, GAO/HAHS 98-72 (Washington, D.C.: U.S. Government Printing Office, March 1998); also see S. Magura and S. Y. Kang, *Validity of Self-Reported Drug Use in High-Risk Populations: A Meta-Analytic Review* (New York: National Development and Research Institute, Inc., 1995).

Note that in DATOS, a quarter of the sample was urine-tested at twelve months, but no criminal checks were done. The DATOS urine sample revealed that those who stayed in treatment fewer than ninety days were more likely to be positive for drugs at one year after discharge. (Fifty-three per-

cent of those staying fewer than ninety days were positive for
any drug one year later, versus 19 percent positive among
those who stayed ninety days or more; 43 percent were positive for cocaine, versus 5 percent, respectively.) A similar
relationship was found for patients in methadone maintenance—those who stayed a year or longer had greater reductions in drug usage during the follow-up period. D. D. Simpson,
G. W. Joe, and B. S. Brown, "Treatment Retention and Follow-
Up Outcomes of the Drug Abuse Treatment Outcome Study,"
Psychology of Addictive Behaviors, vol. 11, no. 4, 1997, pp.
294–307.

Finally, a four-to-five-year follow-up of 2,300 DATOS individuals is in progress, and these subjects have agreed to
provide hair and urine samples for drug testing and to waive
confidentiality of arrest and conviction records. Because self-
reports of drug use within the past year have higher fidelity
than have reports of current use or use within the past month,
researchers contend that total findings of treatment outcome
studies—which question patients about use over the course
of a year or more—are reliable.

• *Inadequate pretreatment and posttreatment assessment.* One expects drug abusers to experience an intensifica-
tion in drug use, psychological symptoms, and life problems
just prior to entering treatment. But this so-called ramping-
up effect virtually ensures that even a poor quality treatment
intervention will appear effective, if only because it breaks
the cycle of addiction at its peak. To compensate for this, some
researchers employ a follow-up technique to capture a longer
and more representative view of pretreatment activity. Thus,
treatment outcome is compared with an average level of pa-
thology antecedent to treatment, rather than with the crisis
that immediately preceded it.

Long follow-up observation periods are also important.
Because there tends to be some decay in benefit following
treatment, too short an observation period could falsely ex-
aggerate the outcome. In addition, since addiction is not an
acute condition, the epidemiologically responsible researcher
monitors patients for years after exposure to treatment, very

much as he would track cancer patients after a course of chemotherapy.

• *High attrition.* Reports of positive outcomes among program graduates are misleading when only a fraction of the patient cohort actually completes the treatment. Similarly, a low rate of follow-up tends, by definition, to include those former patients who are most easily located and, thus, faring best. Difficult-to-find ex-patients are generally the ones who have relapsed, become homeless, or returned to crime.

The large-scale studies mentioned earlier satisfied at least two of these criteria—reasonable follow-up and inclusion of dropouts in the analysis. What they miss by failing to randomize subjects and verify all self-reports they partly amend by using large sample sizes with broad geographic representation. More thorough outcome surveillance—using urine testing and arrest records—can be found in evaluations of addicts who are under the explicit supervision of the criminal justice system.

26. According to ONDCP, there was daily bed capacity for about 150,000 patients (138,000 publicly funded, 10,600 privately funded) in 1996.

27. Outpatient, clinic-based treatment is the most common type of service, with clinics accounting for about 60 percent of all treatment capacity according to the 1996 Uniform Facility Data Set, Office of Applied Studies, Substance Abuse and Mental Health Services Administration, DHHS.

28. According to the American Methadone Treatment Association in New York City, there were 125,000 methadone treatment slots and an estimated 700,000–800,000 heroin addicts in 1997.

29. Residential beds nationwide numbered about 15,000 in 1997, according to Therapeutic Communities of America.

30. Simpson and Sells, "Effectiveness of Treatment for Drug Abuse"; Hubbard et al., *Drug Abuse Treatment*; Simpson and Curry, "Special Issue: Drug Abuse Outcome Study"; Center for Substance and Abuse Treatment, *One Year Later.*

31. De Leon, "Legal Pressure in Therapeutic Communities"; De Leon, Melnick, and Kressel, "Motivation and Readiness

for Therapeutic Community Treatment." Attrition rates in the major studies were high. Among DARP patients, 13 percent completed outpatient treatment, 20 percent completed therapeutic community (TC) treatment, and 28 percent completed methadone maintenance. These high dropout rates were associated with a pattern of readmission to the same or another clinic within a few years. During the twelve-year follow-up period, for example, the average addict in outpatient treatment had 3.4 more treatment admissions; one in a TC had 4.6 more admissions, and one in methadone maintenance had 5.1 more treatment admissions.

Attrition in TOPS and DATOS was also considerable. In TOPS, 8 percent finished a year in outpatient, 12 percent a year in a TC, and 33 percent a year in methadone. Among DATOS patients, about 5 percent finished one year in outpatient, 8 percent in a TC, and 44 percent in methadone. A number of factors likely account for what appears to be a trend toward declining retention; they include the shrinking of adjunct social services provided by the clinic and a higher proportion of cocaine abusers in later studies, and thus fewer patients in all who could benefit from the stabilizing effect of methadone.

The proportion of young patients and multiple-drug abusers—features associated with poorer prognoses—has also increased. In addition, a higher proportion of women in the later studies may also contribute to the attrition trend. Women's notorious skittishness as patients in residential programs is generally attributed to the competing demands of childcare and the distractions of what is often a chaotic family scene. Newer residential programs, therefore, try to accommodate one or more of their children as well. See also D. S. Simpson, G. W. Joe, and B. S. Brown, "Treatment Retention and Follow-Up Outcomes in the Drug Abuse Treatment Outcome Study," *Psychology of Addictive Behaviors*, vol. 11, 1997, pp. 294–307; J. C. Maxwell, "Substance Abuse Trends in Texas, December 1995," in *TCADA Research Briefs*, Texas Commission on Drug and Alcohol Abuse, Austin, Texas, 1996; R. H. Price. and T. D'Aunno, *NIDA III Respondent Report Drug*

Abuse Treatment System Survey: A National Study of the Outpatient Drug-free and Methadone Treatment Systems, 1988–1990 Results (Ann Arbor, Michigan: University of Michigan Institute for Social Research, 1992). Also, see M. D. Anglin and Y. Hser, "Treatment of Drug Abuse," in M. Tonry and J. Q. Wilson, eds., *Drugs and Crime* (Chicago, Illinois: University of Chicago Press, 1990).

32. Dr. David F. Duncan (Brown University, Department of Psychiatry) presented data at the 1997 annual meeting of the Drug Policy Foundation on drug abusers mandated to treatment in Rhode Island. He had found that this group was significantly more likely to designate marijuana as their problem drug, and he expressed concern that these individuals were occupying treatment slots that should more properly go to people addicted to heroin or cocaine, who were on waiting lists for treatment. As of this writing, DATOS researchers are still looking at pretreatment characteristics and outcome by voluntary versus involuntary status. See W. H. McGlothlin, "Criminal Justice Clients," in DuPont, Goldstein, and O'Donnell, *Handbook of Drug Abuse.*

33. McGlothlin, "Criminal Justice Clients."

34. D. R. Gerstein, H. J. Harwood, eds., *Treating Drug Problems*, vol. 1 (Washington, D.C.: Institute of Medicine, National Academy Press, 1990).

35. J. J. Collins and M. Allison, "Legal Coercion and Retention in Drug Abuse Treatment," *Hospital and Community Psychiatry*, vol. 34, 1983, pp. 1145–49; Anglin and Hser, "Treatment of Drug Abuse."

36. A. T. McLellan, I. O. Arndt, D. S. Metzger, G. E. Woody, and C. P. O'Brien, "The Effects of Psychosocial Services in Substance Abuse Treatment," *Journal of the American Medical Association*, vol. 269, no. 15, 1993, pp. 1953–1959; A. T. McLellan, G. R. Grissom, D. Zanis, M. Randall, P. Brill, and C. P. O'Brien, "Problem-Service 'Matching' in Addiction Treatment: A Prospective Study in Four Programs," *Archives of General Psychiatry,* vol. 54, no. 8, 1997, pp. 730–35; Y. Hser, "A Referral System That Matches Drug Users to Treatment Pro-

grams: Existing Research and Relevant Issues," *Journal of Drug Issues*, vol. 25, no. 1, 1995, pp. 209–24.

Indeed, duration of treatment may be more important, and is certainly no less important, than the particular modality. It's true that patients tend to sort themselves out, but with the most severely addicted finding their way into residential treatment, the ratio of outpatient to residential slots is so high that outpatient facilities inevitably serve a rather heterogeneous population. This population includes a sizable percentage of heavily addicted and criminally involved individuals. Indeed, there is considerable similarity between patient outcomes across modalities.

37. J. R. McKay, A. T. McLellan, and A. I. Alterman, "An Evaluation of the Cleveland Criteria for Inpatient Substance Abuse Treatment," *American Journal of Psychiatry*, vol. 149, 1992, pp. 1212–18.

38. S. Nemes, E. Wish, and N. Messina, "The District of Columbia Treatment Initiative," Center for Substance Abuse Research, University of Maryland, College Park, Maryland, 1998.

39. Collins and Allison, "Legal Coercion and Retention in Drug Abuse Treatment."

40. Education and Assistance Corporation, "Brooklyn TASC Predicate Program: A Program Briefing," Carle Place, New York, Education and Assistance Corporation, Criminal Justice Division, 1995.

41. Criminal Justice Policy Council, "Treatment Alternatives to Incarceration Program: An Analysis of Retention and Treatment and Outcome Evaluation," Austin, Texas, Criminal Justice Policy Council, 1995.

42. M. D. Anglin, D. Longshore, S. Turner, D. McBride, J. Inciardi, and M. Prendergast, "Studies of the Functioning and Effectiveness of Treatment Alternatives to Street Crime," Final Report, UCLA Drug Research Center, 1996.

43. F. S. Taxman, "Reducing Recidivism through a Seamless System of Care: Components of Effective Treatment, Supervision, and Transition Services in the Community," Col-

lege Park, Maryland, 1998 (paper prepared for the Office of National Drug Control Policy Conference on Treatment and the Criminal Justice System, February 20, 1998). "Felony Defendants in Large Urban Counties in 1992," Bureau of Justice Statistics (NCJ-148826), 1995.

44. National Center on Addiction and Substance Abuse at Columbia University, *Behind Bars: Substance Abuse and America's Prison Population* (New York, 1998), p. 127; C. W. Harlow, *Profile of Jail Inmates, 1996,* Bureau of Justice Statistics (NCJ-164620), 1998; "Prisoners in 1996," in *Bureau of Justice Statistics Bulletin*, June 1997.

An arrestee who participated in Drug Use Forecasting in 1990 was considered to be probably in need of drug treatment if he or she tested positive for one of the drugs and met one of the following conditions: (1) reported frequent use of the drug (at least ten times in the past month); (2) reported being dependent on the drug at some time in the past; (3) reported being currently in treatment; or (4) reported being in need of treatment. According to this definition, the percentage of arrestees who were probably in need of treatment was 45 percent of those who tested positive for cocaine, 59 percent of those who tested positive for opiates, 10 percent of those who tested positive for amphetamines, and 77 percent of those who tested positive for cocaine, opiates, or amphetamines and who reported injection drug use. From Prendergast et al., "Drug Treatment Need among Offender Populations."

45. G. R. Speckart and M. D. Anglin, "Narcotics and Crime: A Causal Modeling Approach, *Journal of Quantitative Criminology*, vol. 2, 1986, pp. 3–28; D. N. Nurco, T. W. Kinlock, and T. E. Hanlon, "The Drugs-Crime Connection," in J. A. Inciardi, ed., *Handbook of Drug Control in the United States* (Westport, Connecticut: Greenwood Press, 1990), pp.71–90; M. R. Chaiken, "Crime Rates and Substance Abuse among Types of Offenders," in B. D. Johnson and E. Wish, eds., *Crime Rates among Drug-Abusing Offenders: Final Report to the National Institute of Justice* (New York: Narcotic and Drug Research, Inc., 1986). For a detailed discussion of the history and effec-

tiveness of TASC, see M. D. Anglin, D. Longshore, S. Turner, D. McBride, J. Inciardi, and M. Prendergast, *Studies of the Functioning and Effectiveness of Treatment Alternatives to Street Crime (TASC) Programs*, Final Report, UCLA Drug Abuse Research Center, Los Angeles, California, 1996. Also, see Taxman, "Reducing Recidivism through a Seamless System."

46. "The arrangement of the judge at the center of the operation reflects the growing desire of judges to have more control," says Judge Jeffrey Tauber, president and founder of the National Association of Drug Court Professionals. This may be one reason why TASC programs have declined, while drug courts have expanded. (From personal communication, August 1997.)

47. S. Belenko, "Research on Drug Courts," *National Drug Court Institute Review*, vol. 1, no. 1, 1998, pp.1–44.

48. Experimental designs are difficult to implement. Researchers associated with the Brooklyn Treatment Court in New York are comparing its participants with matched offenders from neighboring areas who do not have access to drug court but who would choose that option if it were available. This avoids introducing the confounding variable of motivation, a problem intrinsic to studies that compare individuals who choose drug court with those who actively reject it. But perhaps the most clinically informative comparison, which has yet to be conducted, would include drug court participants with matched patients who were court-referred to the same treatment program. This would help tease apart the combined effects of sanctions and heavy judicial supervision from the influence of treatment.

49. U.S. General Accounting Office, *Drug Courts: Overview of Growth, Characteristics and Results* (Washington, D.C.: U.S. General Accounting Office, 1997).

50. C. A. Cooper, S. R. Bartlett, M. A. Shaw, and K. K. Yang, "Drug Courts: 1997 Overview of Operational Characteristics and Implementation Issues," vol. 1, Office of Justice Programs Drug Court Clearinghouse and Technical Assistance Project, American University, May 1997; S. Satel, "Do Drug Courts Really Work?" *City Journal*, Summer 1998, pp. 81–87.

51. Bureau of Justice Statistics Special Report, "Recidivism of Felons on Probation, 1986–1989," U.S. Department of Justice, Office of Justice Programs, 1992.

52. M. Finigan, "An Outcome Program Evaluation of the Multnomah County S.T.O.P. Drug Diversion Program," prepared by the State Justice Institute of Alexandria, Virginia, for the Multnomah County, Oregon, Department of Corrections, January 6, 1998.

53. E. P. Deschenes, S. Turner, P. W. Greenwood, and J. Chiesa, "An Experimental Evaluation of Drug Testing and Treatment Interventions for Probationers in Maricopa County, Arizona," prepared for the National Institute of Justice by RAND, July 1996.

54. W. C. Terry III, "Broward County's Dedicated Drug Treatment Court: From Post-Adjudication to Diversion," in Terry, ed., *Judicial Change and Drug Treatment Courts: Case Studies in Innovation* (Beverly Hills, California: Sage, 1998).

55. J. S. Goldkamp and D. Weiland, *Assessing the Impact of Dade County's Felony Drug Court: Final Report to the National Institute of Justice* (Philadelphia, Pennsylvania: Criminal and Justice Research Institute, 1993).

56. A. Harrell and S. Cavanaugh, *Preliminary Results from the Evaluation of the D.C. Superior Court Drug Intervention Program for Drug Felony Defendants* (Washington, D.C.: Urban Institute, 1997).

57. Office of Justice Programs, *OJP Drugs and Crime and CASA behind Bars 1998*, Appendix D; Working group, Department of Justice, *A Report to the Assistant Attorney General, January 1996.*

58. National Institute of Justice, "Evaluation of Drug Treatment in Local Corrections," prepared by the National Council on Crime and Delinquency, 1996. This report concluded that there was a "modest positive effect on the probability of recidivism" based on a review of five programs. The importance of aftercare services is stressed, because the length of treatment is limited by the offenders' relatively short stays in jail. Authors cite other studies showing that the effects of in-jail treatment tend to wane over time, but short-term out-

come seems to be enhanced with longer time in treatment and participation in aftercare.

59. Douglas S. Lipton, National Drug Research Institute, New York City; personal communication, July 6, 1998.

60. G. P. Falkin, H. K. Wexler, and D. S. Lipton, "Drug Treatment in State Prisons," in D. R. Gerstein and H. J. Harwood, eds., *Treating Drug Problems*, vol. 2 (Washington, D.C.: National Academy Press, Institute of Medicine, 1990).

61. J. A. Inciardi, S. S. Martin, C. A. Butzin, R. M. Hooper, and L. D. Harrison, "An Effective Model of Prison-Based Treatment for Drug-Involved Offenders," *Journal of Drug Issues,* vol. 27, no. 2, 1997, pp. 261–78. The effectiveness of drug treatment in jails is less well characterized.

62. D. Young, "Bridging Drug Treatment and Criminal Justice," Vera Institute of Justice, New York, New York, 1996.

63. M. A. R. Kleiman, "Coerced Abstinence: A Neo-Paternalistic Drug Policy Initiative," in L. M. Mead, ed., *The New Paternalism: Supervisory Approaches to Poverty* (Washington, D.C.: Brookings Institution Press, 1997).

64. National Center on Addiction and Substance Abuse at Columbia University, *Behind Bars: Substance Abuse and America's Prison Population*; Harlow, *Profile of Jail Inmates, 1996*; "Prisoners in 1996," in *Bureau of Justice Statistics Bulletin*, June 1997; F. Taxman, and J. M. Byrne, "Locating Absconders: Results from a Randomized Failed Experiment," *Federal Probation,* vol. 58, 1994, pp.13–23; P. A. Langan and M. A. Cunniff, "Recidivism of Felons on Probation, 1986–1989," *Bureau of Justice Statistics Special Report* (Washington, D.C.: U.S. Bureau of Justice Statistics, 1993).

65. Harrell and Cavanaugh, *Preliminary Results from D.C. Superior Court.*

66. Note that even the standard track was under drug court monitoring, with frequent urine testings, judicial praise or censure, and the threat of incarceration (at the end of six months) if the record of test results were poor. Thus the standard track was not the equivalent of a placebo control. The standard-track individuals were under much closer supervision than were typical probationers. Kleiman also points out

that millions of people who use illicit drugs have minimal addictive potential—especially with regard to marijuana and hallucinogens. Technically, they are not "drug addicts." For many of them social rehabilitation may well be warranted, but drug treatment itself should be reserved for the truly addicted. Personal communication with M. A. R. Kleiman, June 21, 1998.

67. The State of Connecticut passed a bill in May 1998, the Zero Tolerance Drug Supervision Program, that would drastically cut prison time for nonviolent drug and nondrug offenders, on the condition that they undergo testing for drug use. Offenders who served at least half of a two-to-four–year sentence may be tested up to three times per week, and whenever a urine test is positive they will be detained for two days in a halfway house. Repeated failures will result in return to prison. Legislators estimate that incarceration costs $25,000 a year, while the drug testing program will cost $3,000 plus the cost of probation services. State representative Robert Farr, the bill's author, told the *New York Times*, "in our parole programs a substantial number of our people are using drugs. Now for the first time, we're saying there will be consequences."

In July 1998, Maryland's twenty-four jurisdictions implemented a program called Break the Cycle of Crime and Addiction, part of a multistate testing, sanctions, and drug-treatment demonstration program supported by the ONDCP and the Department of Justice. Sanctions policy in Maryland involved imposing a consequence for each positive test, ensuring swift (within twenty-four hours), certain, and progressively severe responses, in addition to rewarding abstinence and compliance.

Coerced abstinence has been adopted at the federal level, first as a Clinton administration proposal in 1996, then as a law passed by Congress requiring every state to create a program of testing and sanctions for drug-involved offenders as a condition of receiving federal prison-building grants. The implementation effected in 1999 applies, unfortunately, only to prisoners and parolees, not probationers.

68. R. E. Peterson, *Drug Enforcement Works* (New York: O'Grady Press, 1997). Also see Michigan Office of Drug Control Policy, "Zero Tolerance Offender Treatment Quarterly Report" (available through Michigan Office of Drug Control Policy, Lansing, Michigan; phone, 517-373-4700).

69. Kleiman, "Coerced Abstinence."

70. Gerstein and Harwood, *Treating Drug Problems*.

71. J. Sullum, "Drug Test," *Reason Magazine*, March 1998, pp. 22–31; A. I. Leshner, "Addiction Is a Brain Disease, and It Matters," *Science,* vol. 278, 1997, p. 45; Consensus Statement, Physician Leadership on National Drug Policy, July 9, 1997. See also "Medical News and Perspective," in *Journal of the American Medical Association*, 1997, vol. 278, no. 5, p. 378; Bill Moyers, "Addiction: Close to Home," on Public Broadcasting Service, March 29–31, 1998.

72. Psychologist Gene M. Heyman of Harvard University points to epidemiologic data to show that relapse is not universal among addicts. The large Epidemiologic Catchment Area (ECA) study, funded by the National Institute of Mental Health, shows that in the general population, remission rates are the norm, not the exception. According to ECA criteria for remission—defined as no symptoms for the year just prior to the interview—59 percent of roughly 1,300 respondents who met lifetime criteria were free of drug problems. The average duration of remission was 2.7 years and the mean duration of illness was 6.1 years, with most cases (75th percentile) lasting no more than 8 years. Furthermore, the addicts most likely to serve as subjects in treatment-outcome studies—treatment seekers—form a subgroup of the general addict population that is most prone to relapse. While roughly only one-third of drug abusers seek treatment, more than 60 percent of them are diagnosed with additional psychiatric disorders, according to the National Co-Morbidity Study. Among abusers who have not sought treatment, however, about 29 percent have additional psychiatric diagnoses, a proportion not much different from the prevalence of psychiatric illness in the general population. Also see S. Satel, "The Fallacies of No-Fault Addiction," *Public Interest*, Winter 1999.

73. Anglin also reports that the vast majority who enter voluntarily do not intend to use treatment to become abstinent, but rather to reduce drug use to manageable levels. For a discussion of coercion and alcohol treatment see C. M. Weisner, "Appendix D: Coercion in Alcohol Treatment," in *Broadening the Base of Treatment for Alcohol Problems* (Washington, D.C.: National Academy Press, Institute of Medicine, 1990). Also, see M. D. Anglin, M. Brecht, and E. Maddahian, "Pretreatment Characteristics and Treatment Performance of Legally Coerced vs. Voluntary Methadone Maintenance Admissions," *Criminology,* vol. 27, 1989, pp. 537–57. See also A. T. McLellan and C. Weisner, "Achieving the Public Health and Safety Potential of Substance Abuse Treatments," in W. K. Bickel and R. J. DeGrandpre, eds., *Drug Policy and Human Nature* (New York: Plenum Press, 1996).

74. Group for the Advancement of Psychiatry, "Coercion by Employers to Combat Substance Abuse," in *Group for the Advancement of Psychiatry Report,* no. 137, 1994; Group for the Advancement of Psychiatry, *Forced into Treatment: The Role of Coercion in Clinical Practice* (Washington, D.C.: American Psychiatric Press, 1994).

75. P. B. Beaumont and S. J. Allsop, "An Industrial Alcohol Policy: The Characteristics of Worker Success," *British Journal of Addiction*, vol. 79, 1984, pp. 315–18.

76. D. C. Walsh, R. W. Hingson, D. M. Merrigan, S. M. Levenson, L. A. Cupples, T. Heeren, G. A. Coffman, C. A. Becker, T. A. Barker, S. K. Hamilton, T. G. McGuire, and C. A. Kelly, "A Randomized Trial of Treatment Options for Alcohol-Abusing Workers," *New England Journal of Medicine*, vol. 325, 1991, pp. 775–82. N.B.: The authors conclude that for employed problem drinkers, initial referral alone to Alcoholics Anonymous or to a choice of programs, although less costly than inpatient care, involves more risk than does compulsory inpatient treatment and should be accompanied by close monitoring for signs of incipient relapse (within the first six months). Individuals not assigned to inpatient care were more likely to be rehospitalized.

77. E. Lawental, A. T. McLellan, et al., "Coerced Treatment

for Substance Abuse Problems Detected through Workplace Urine Surveillance: Is It Effective?" *Journal of Substance Abuse Treatment*, vol. 8, no. 1, 1996, pp. 115–28.

78. Dennis Saffran, Center for the Community Interest, New York. (From personal communication, August 13, 1998.)

79. Alphonso Jackson; personal communication, May 1998.

80. F. Seigel, "Homeless Advocates' Impure Motives," *New York Post*, March 30, 1997.

81. P. Hellman, "Justice Freedman v. New York," *City Journal,* Spring 1997, pp. 56–65.

82. American Civil Liberties Union, "ACLU Urges Congress to Reject Moves to Encourage More Workplace Drug Testing," press release, May 14, 1998.

83. National Committee to Prevent Child Abuse, "The Relationship between Parental Alcohol or Other Problems and Child Maltreatment," Fact Sheet no. 14, September 1996. Available from website http://www.childabuse.org/fs14.html.

84. Legal Action Center, New York, "Making Welfare Reform Work: Tools for Confronting Alcohol and Drug Problems among Welfare Recipients," September 1997.

85. P. M. Miller, "A Behavioral Intervention Program for Chronic Public Drunkenness Offenders," *Archives of General Psychiatry*, vol. 32, 1975, pp. 915–18.

86. S. T. Higgins, J. W. Tidey, and M. L. Stitzer, "Community Reinforcement and Contingency Management in the Treatment of Alcohol, Cocaine, and Opioid Dependence," in A. W. Graham and T. K. Schultz, eds., *American Society of Addiction Medicine Principles of Addiction Medicine,* 2nd ed. (Chevy Chase, Md.: American Society of Addiction Medicine, Inc., 1998), pp. 675–90.

87. S. T. Higgins, D. D. Delaney, A. J. Budney, W. K. Bickel, J. R. Hughes, F. Foerg, and J. W. Fenwick, "A Behavioral Approach to Achieving Initial Cocaine Abstinence," *American Journal of Psychiatry,* vol. 148, 1991, pp. 1218–24; S. T. Higgins, A. J. Budney, W. K. Bickel, J. R. Hughes, F. Foerg, and G. J. Badger, "Achieving Cocaine Abstinence with a Behavioral Approach," *American Journal of Psychiatry,* vol. 150, 1993, pp. 763–69; S. T. Higgins, A. J. Budney, W. K. Bickel, F. E. Foerg,

R. Donham, and G. J. Badger, "Incentives Improve Treatment Retention and Cocaine Abstinence in Ambulatory Cocaine Patients," *Archives of General Psychiatry*, vol. 51, 1994, pp. 568–76.

88. K. Silverman, S. T. Higgins, R. K. Brooner, I. D. Montoya, E. J. Cone, C. R. Schuster, and K. L. Preston, "Sustained Cocaine Abstinence in Methadone Maintenance Patients through Voucher-Based Reinforcement Therapy," *Archives of General Psychiatry*, vol. 53, 1996, pp. 409–15.

89. K. Silverman, M. A. D. Chutuape, G. E. Bigelow, and M. L. Stitzer, "Reinforcement of Cocaine Abstinence in Treatment Resistant Patients: Effects of Reinforcer Magnitude," in L. S. Harris, ed., *College on the Problems of Drug Dependence,* NIDA Research Monograph no. 174, NIH pub. No. 97-4236 (Washington, D.C.: Government Printing Office, 1996), p. 74.

90. In this study, the authors studied twenty-nine intravenous cocaine-abusing patients, many also HIV-positive, who failed the standard CM voucher schedule that permitted them to earn up to $1,155 in vouchers exchangeable for goods and services. The research team then ran these individuals through three separate nine-week voucher conditions: zero, low- ($382), and high- ($3,480) magnitude, depending on the total value of vouchers that could be earned. Patients were randomized to the various voucher sequences: that is, high-zero-low, low-high-zero, and so forth.

91. J. B. Milby, J. E. Schumacher, J. M. Racsynski, E. Caldwell, M. Engle, M. Michael, and J. Carr, "Sufficient Conditions for Effective Treatment of Substance-Abusing Homeless Persons," *Drug and Alcohol Dependence,* vol. 43, 1996, pp. 23–38.

92. R. K. Reis and K. A. Comtois, "Managing Disability Benefits as Part of Treatment for Persons with Severe Mental Illness and Co-Morbid Alcohol and Drug Disorders," *American Journal of Addictions* (forthcoming).

93. R. A. Rosenheck, director, Northeast Program Evaluation Center, Veterans Administration Medical Center; personal communication, January 1998.

94. Thus far, only South Carolina's high court has upheld

the legality of charging child endangerment, but state supreme courts in Florida, Kentucky, Nevada, Ohio, and Wisconsin, as well as many lower courts, have struck such charges down, often narrowly ruling that a viable fetus was not a person under the particular criminal law invoked. Alcohol has been the subject of debate as well, and on July 1, 1998, South Dakota became the first state to allow judges to order pregnant women who abuse alcohol into treatment. State legislators were moved to enact the law because of the high prevalence of fetal alcohol syndrome, which in some parts of South Dakota is greater than twenty times the national average of 1 in 500 live births. One of the statutes within the law makes drinking while pregnant a form of child abuse.

Not surprisingly, this practice sparked women's rights and civil liberties groups to accuse lawmakers of criminalizing pregnancy (a status, rather than a crime) and thus violating women's constitutional rights to due process. Because the crack "epidemic" involved an especially high number of women of childbearing age, rights activists claimed that "criminalizing pregnancy" via child protection laws disproportionately affected women. At the same time, rights groups have called for more treatment, correctly pointing out that treatment slots for pregnant women are scarce and that some methadone programs will discharge a woman who becomes pregnant. Because almost all the South Carolina women involved in coerced treatment were black (as are most of the hospitals' indigent obstetrical patients), allegations of racism and violation of privacy rights were made against the heavily federally funded Medical University of South Carolina. The furor caused the university to discontinue its program in 1994, under pressure from the U.S. Department of Health and Human Services. A policy statement from the physicians' organization, the American Society for Addiction Medicine, expresses a view typical of the public health establishment: "The imposition of criminal penalties solely because a person suffers from an illness (addiction) is inappropriate and counterproductive. Criminal prosecution of chemically dependent women will have the overall result of deterring them from seeking . . . care, thus increasing harm to children and society as a whole."

95. E. O. Horger, S. B. Brown, and C. M. Condon, "Cocaine in Pregnancy: Confronting the Problem," *Journal of the South Carolina Medical Association,* vol. 86, 1990, pp. 527–31.

96. Ibid.

97. Center for Reproductive Law and Policy, New York; Lindesmith Center, New York.

98. For a discussion of the possible negative consequences of coercion, see R. S. Schottenfeld, "Involuntary Treatment of Substance Abuse Disorders—Impediments to Success," *Psychiatry,* vol. 52, 1989, pp. 1640–76. Civil commitment and diversion programs are expensive to implement effectively. (Personal communication from Jerome Jaffe, MD, former director of the Special Action Office for Drug Abuse Prevention under President Nixon.) J. J. Platt concluded that such programs are typically effective only if the heroin abuser is placed on long-term probation or parole (five to ten years), with close supervision, regular urine testing, and a realistic threat of reincarceration for serious instances of relapse. J. J. Platt, *Heroin Addiction: Theory, Research and Treatment,* vol. 2, *The Addict, the Treatment Process, and Social Control* (Malabar, Florida: Krieger, 1995).

99. P. A. Galon and R. A. Liebelt, "Involuntary Treatment of Substance Abuse Disorders," in M. R. Munetz, ed., *Can Mandatory Treatment Be Therapeutic?* New Directions for Mental Health Services, no. 75 (San Francisco: Jossey-Bass Publishers, Fall 1997).

100. This was the type of rationale described by psychologist Barbara Lex at McLean Hospital in Boston, who examined data for 500 women civilly committed to treatment in Massachusetts in 1995. Except for the severity of the condition precipitating commitment, these women were demographically similar to a comparison set of women who were voluntarily admitted. The committed group stayed in treatment an average of four times longer. B. W. Lex, "Women Civilly Committed to Substance Abuse Treatments in Massachusetts," data presented at the American Society of

Addiction Medicine, 29th annual meeting, New Orleans, Louisiana, 1998.

101. Taxman and Byrne, "Locating Absconders"; Langan and Cunliffe, "Recidivism of Felons on Probation."

102. S. Belenko, G. Nikerson, and T. Rubinstein, *Crack and the New York Courts: A Study of Judicial Responses and Attitudes* (New York: New York City Criminal Justice Agency, 1990). This study examined perceptions affecting judges' decisions regarding the adjudication of crack and powdered cocaine offenders. Most of them believed that only motivated defendants would benefit from treatment.

About the Author

Sally L. Satel is a practicing psychiatrist and lecturer at the Yale University School of Medicine. She is a staff psychiatrist at the Oasis Clinic and a senior associate at the Ethics and Public Policy Center, both in Washington, D.C.

Dr. Satel has written widely on drug treatment. In addition to medical journals, her articles have appeared in the *New Republic*, the *City Journal* (of the Manhattan Institute), the *Los Angeles Times*, the *Wall Street Journal*, the *New York Times*, *SLATE*, the *Public Interest*, and the *Women's Quarterly*. Of particular interest to her are the problems of politicized science and the intrusions of political correctness into medicine and research.

Dr. Satel did her undergraduate work at Cornell University and received an M.S. degree from the University of Chicago. She received her M.D. from Brown University and completed residency training in psychiatry at the Yale University School of Medicine.